Access to History

Charles V: Ruler, Dynast and Defender of the Faith, 1500–58

D0256132

Access to History

General Editor: Keith Randell

Charles V: Ruler, Dynast and Defender of the Faith, 1500–58

Stewart MacDonald

Hodder & Stoughton

A MEMBER OF THE HODDER HEADLINE GROUP

The cover illustration shows the painting *Charles V at the Battle of Mühlberg* by Titian, 1547 (Courtesy Museo del Prado, Madrid/Ampliaciones y Reproducciones "MAS").

Some other titles in the series:

Luther and the German Reformation, 1517–55   ISBN 0 340 51808 1
Keith Randell

John Calvin and the Later Reformation   ISBN 0 340 52940 7
Keith Randell

The Catholic and Counter Reformations   ISBN 0 340 53495 8
Keith Randell

Spain: Rise and Decline, 1474–1643   ISBN 0 340 51807 3
Jill Kilsby

Henry VII   ISBN 0 340 53801 5
Caroline Rogers

Henry VIII and the Government of England   ISBN 0 340 55325 1
Keith Randell

British Library Cataloguing in Publication Data
MacDonald, Stewart
  Charles V: ruler, dynast and defender of the
  faith, 1500–58. – (Access to history)
  I. Title   II. Series
  946.0092

  ISBN 0–340–53558–X

First published 1992
Impression number 10   9   8   7   6   5   4   3
Year   1998   1997   1996   1995   1994

Copyright © 1992 Stewart MacDonald

Typeset by Wearset, Boldon, Tyne & Wear
Printed in Great Britain for Hodder & Stoughton Educational, a division of Hodder Headline Plc, 338 Euston Road, London NW1 3BH by Page Bros, Norwich.

Contents

iv   Contents

Preface

To the general reader

Although the *Access to History* series has been designed with the needs of students studying the subject at higher examination levels very much in mind, it also has a great deal to offer the general reader. The main body of the text (i.e. ignoring the Study Guides at the ends of chapters) forms a readable and yet stimulating survey of a coherent topic as studied by historians. However, each author's aim has not merely been to provide a clear explanation of what happened in the past (to interest and inform): it has also been assumed that most readers wish to be stimulated into thinking further about the topic and to form opinions of their own about the significance of the events that are described and discussed (to be challenged). Thus, although no prior knowledge of the topic is expected on the reader's part, she or he is treated as an intelligent and thinking person throughout. The author tends to share ideas and possibilities with the reader, rather than passing on numbers of so-called 'historical truths'.

To the student reader

There are many ways in which the series can be used by students studying History at a higher level. It will, therefore, be worthwhile thinking about your own study strategy before you start your work on this book. Obviously, your strategy will vary depending on the aim you have in mind, and the time for study that is available to you.

If, for example, you want to acquire a general overview of the topic in the shortest possible time, the following approach will probably be the most effective:

1 Read chapter 1 and think about its contents.
2 Read the 'Making notes' section at the end of chapter 2 and decide whether it is necessary for you to read this chapter.
3 If it is, read the chapter, stopping at each heading or ★ to note down the main points that have been made.
4 Repeat stage 2 (and stage 3 where appropriate) for all the other chapters.

If, however, your aim is to gain a thorough grasp of the topic, taking however much time is necessary to do so, you may benefit from carrying out the same procedure with each chapter, as follows:

1 Read the chapter as fast as you can, and preferably at one sitting.
2 Study the flow diagram at the end of the chapter, ensuring that you understand the general 'shape' of what you have just read.

3   Read the 'Making notes' section (and the 'Answering essay questions' section, if there is one) and decide what further work you need to do on the chapter. In particularly important sections of the book, this will involve reading the chapter a second time and stopping at each heading and * to think about (and to write a summary of) what you have just read.

4   Attempt the 'Source-based questions' section. It will sometimes be sufficient to think through your answers, but additional understanding will often be gained by forcing yourself to write them down.

When you have finished the main chapters of the book, study the 'Further Reading' section and decide what additional reading (if any) you will do on the topic.

This book has been designed to help make your studies both enjoyable and successful. If you can think of ways in which this could have been done more effectively, please write to tell me. In the meantime, I hope that you will gain greatly from your study of History.

Keith Randell

CHAPTER 1

Introduction to the Reign of Charles V

One of the most memorable episodes of sixteenth-century European history took place in the Netherlands on 25 October 1555. One of Europe's most powerful rulers, the Emperor Charles V, made public his decision to abdicate and to retire from political life. His dominions were extensive; the New World in the Americas, Spain, the Netherlands, Germany and parts of Italy. No other prince in Christendom had territories on anything like this scale. The announcement was made at a moving and carefully stage-managed ceremony in the Parliament Hall of the Ducal Palace in Brussels. Debilitated by gout and prematurely aged at 55, the Emperor arrived at the palace on a small mule; he was no longer fit enough to ride a horse. He was soberly dressed in black. The hall was overflowing with the nobles and dignitaries of the Netherlands. He was helped to a raised throne at the end of the hall, accompanied by many of his close relatives. The Emperor remained seated while it was announced, to the astonishment of the assembly, that he wished to renounce his worldly titles. He was then helped to his feet and, putting on his glasses to consult his notes, he made his famous valedictory speech to his subjects. He recalled the many journeys he had made, resulting in long absences from his native Netherlands. He apologised to his people for the incessant wars of his reign and assured them that his goal had always been the peace of Christendom. He gave thanks to God for his constant support and commended his subjects to protect the Church and to root out all heresy. Most poignantly, he made apology for his weaknesses and failings and asked for the forgiveness of his subjects. Of his son and heir Philip, he said, 'I trust that God will grant him the talents and the strength to fulfil, better than I have done, the obligations imposed upon a king.' Returning to his seat pale and exhausted, Charles was embraced by his tearful son. Witnesses reported sobbing throughout the hall.

1 Charles' Inheritance

Charles V's rule began 40 years earlier when he inherited the Netherlands in 1515. Over the next four years he inherited the rest of his numerous dominions. His lands were bestowed upon him through a complex line of inheritance. Through his father he was a member of the Habsburg dynasty, which rose to power in Austria in the late thirteenth century. Charles' Habsburg ancestors, the archdukes of Austria, had acquired a patchwork of territories in central Europe; Austria, Styria, Tyrol, Carinthia and Carniola (see map on page 21). However, the

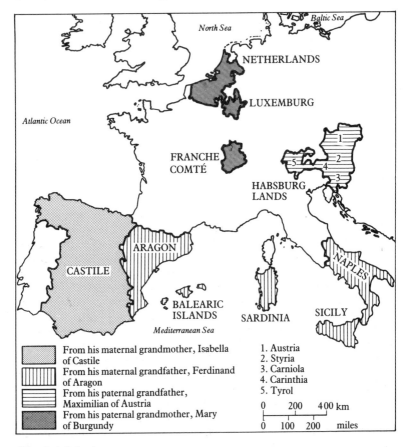

Map legend:

From his maternal grandmother, Isabella of Castile

From his maternal grandfather, Ferdinand of Aragon

From his paternal grandfather, Maximilian of Austria

From his paternal grandmother, Mary of Burgundy

1. Austria
2. Styria
3. Carniola
4. Carinthia
5. Tyrol

0   200   400 km

0   100   200   miles

Charles' Inheritance

dynasty had been weakened by family quarrels and the division of the inheritance, until its fortunes recovered significantly when Charles' grandfather, Maximilian, married into the rich and powerful House of Burgundy in 1477. The Burgundian alliance, together with the substantial territories of the Habsburgs in central Europe, guaranteed the dynasty a prominent role in Europe. When Maximilian died in 1519 his only son was already 13 years dead. So Charles succeeded to the Habsburg lands in central Europe. However, Habsburg princes had, since 1438, become accustomed to inheriting more than just the family's hereditary lands. The strength of the Habsburg power-base in central Europe had enabled a succession of Austrian archdukes to gain the elective title of Holy Roman Emperor. The title was conferred on the candidate who won a majority of votes among seven of Germany's leading princes. The Emperor ruled Germany. The imperial title added greatly to the prestige of the Habsburgs. Firstly, by bringing Germany

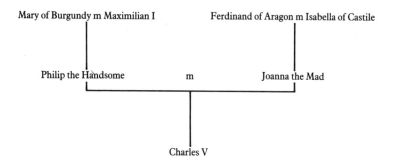

Charles V's antecedents

and the Austrian lands together under a single dynastic authority, it made the Habsburgs the dominant power in central Europe. Secondly, the holder of the title was deemed, by long tradition, to be the secular head of Christendom, just as the Pope was its spiritual leader. Charles succeeded Maximilian as Holy Roman Emperor in 1519 and continued the Habsburg monopoly of the title which lasted until 1806.

Earlier, in 1515, Charles had inherited the Burgundian lands, mainly made up of the Netherlands. This resulted from his grandfather Maximilian's marriage, in 1477, to Mary of Burgundy, the heiress to the Netherlands. Mary and Maximilian had ruled the country jointly until Mary's death in 1482. In 1478 Mary had given birth to a son Philip. Maximilian had recognised his son as head of state in the Netherlands in 1494 (he came to be known as Philip the Handsome). In 1496 Philip married the Spanish princess, Joanna, and in 1500 she gave birth to the future Charles V. Therefore, when Philip died suddenly in 1506, Charles, as his eldest son, was declared titular head of state. In 1515 he was declared of age as ruler of the Netherlands. The Netherlands was a conglomeration of territories now occupied by the present-day Netherlands and Belgium, together with some surrounding territories (see map, page 15). Its rulers called themselves the Dukes of Burgundy. However, in 1477 the French had seized the province of Burgundy, the ancestral lands of the Burgundian dukes. Henceforth the Burgundian dukes ruled the Netherlands but the family lands from which they derived their name were retained by the French.

The final part of Charles' patrimony was Spain. Spain was not a single political entity. It comprised the kingdom of Castile, the most important realm, and the kingdom of Aragon. The latter contained the lesser kingdoms of Catalonia and Valencia (see map, page 23). When Charles' father, Philip of Burgundy, married the daughter of Ferdinand of Aragon and Queen Isabella of Castile in 1496, the Spanish prospects for the House of Habsburg did not appear promising. Joanna was only the fourth in line to the kingdoms of Spain. However, the early deaths of the other heirs paved the way for Joanna and Philip's succession.

They succeeded firstly to Castile, when Joanna's mother Isabella died in 1504. The Castilians were suspicious of the Aragonese, and Joanna's father was obliged to stand aside. However, Philip died in 1506 at the age of 28, precipitating a mental breakdown in Joanna. Ferdinand was invited to govern Castile as well as his own kingdom of Aragon until Philip and Joanna's eldest son, Charles, came of age. Charles was now set to inherit Castile, as long as his mother remained unfit to govern, and Aragon, when his grandfather Ferdinand died. However, in 1509 he appeared close to losing his Aragonese inheritance. In that year Ferdinand had a son by a second marriage, but the new heir lived only for a few hours. Therefore, when Ferdinand died in 1516 Charles claimed the right to rule both Castile and Aragon. In Spain he became known as King Charles I, although in European history he is usually known by his imperial title, Emperor Charles V.

2 Charles' Upbringing and Character

Charles was born in the town of Ghent in the Netherlands on 24 February 1500. His native language was French. The young prince was brought up in the Netherlands with his three sisters, under the care of his aunt, Margaret of Austria. He did not meet his mother until 1517, when he travelled to Spain to take up his inheritance there. Historians have been most interested in those aspects of his youth which provide clues to an understanding of his later behaviour as a ruler. They invariably focus upon three aspects of his upbringing; his religious instruction, his schooling in the arts of chivalry and his education in affairs of state.

In religious matters Charles' teacher was Adrian of Utrecht, who was to become Pope Adrian VI in 1522. Adrian had a profound influence on Charles and instilled in him a genuine devotion to the Church and an austere and pious code of personal behaviour. Charles grew up attending mass and confession regularly and with a sound knowledge of the teachings of the Church. The Burgundian court of Charles' youth was very much steeped in the traditions of chivalry. Chivalry was the social code of knighthood. The ideal of chivalry was the gallant and honourable Christian knight. In his youth Charles was an enthusiastic student of the skills of knighthood; riding, hunting and jousting. He learned to appreciate the pomp and ceremony of court life which provided the social environment of knighthood; banqueting, balls and assorted court pageantry. Therefore, against this chivalric background, Charles grew up to value the knightly qualities of honour, dignity, daring and glory. Lastly, Charles was carefully instructed in public affairs from an early age. When he inherited the title of the Duke of Burgundy at the age of six he was expected to carry out the official functions of his office, such as conferring knighthoods upon his subjects. At the age of nine his education in the affairs of state became

Charles with a hunting dog, 1532–by Jakob Seisenegger

the responsibility of the Burgundian noble, Chièvres de Croy. Chièvres worked hard to impress on his charge both political ambition and a sense of duty in state affairs. The study of history played an important part in the prince's education. Through it he was taught to revere the achievements of his ancestors and to feel a sense of responsibility towards his dynastic inheritance. However, in his youth at least, Charles was a somewhat reluctant student of state affairs, preferring the excitement of the hunt and the tournament.

To what extent, then, did Charles' early experiences in the Netherlands stamp his character and outlook for the rest of his life? There is abundant evidence that his deep religious feelings remained fundamental to his whole existence. He attended mass twice daily, listened to readings from the Bible and often discussed his spiritual welfare with his confessors. Before any major political or military enterprise he spent long hours in prayer. One of the most striking aspects of his religious outlook was his unshakeable belief in God's direction of human affairs. This was, of course, the received theological wisdom of the time; human life unfolded only according to God's divine, if often inscrutable, plan. In Charles this belief in divine control of human destiny was particularly deep-rooted. It lent to his character a strong forbearance and fatalism in the face of adversity. No matter how badly things appeared to be going for the Emperor, he put his faith in God's wisdom and judgement. Writing to his brother Ferdinand in 1541, for example, he reflected on his military disaster at Algiers:

> We must thank God for all and hope that after this disaster He will grant us of His great goodness some great good fortune . . . It was essential not so much to rise early, as to rise at the right time, and God alone could judge what that time should be.

Similar comments occur frequently in the Emperor's correspondence. Perhaps it was such a faith in God's ultimate wisdom that enabled him to conduct himself with the self-control and detachment that many historians have commented upon. Throughout his reign he confronted his many trials with remarkable forbearance. His advice to his son Philip reflected one of the merits of his own character: 'In your bearing be calm and reserved. Say nothing in anger.'

The religion of the Netherlands, and of Adrian of Utrecht in particular, strongly upheld the virtues of a stern and pious code of personal behaviour. This left its mark on Charles' adult character. He was not fond of small-talk or laughter. He disapproved of 'unseemly jokes' and drunkenness. In dress he was modest and plain. By the standards of the European rulers of his day, Charles was distinctly restrained in his sexual conduct. As far as can be ascertained he remained faithful to his wife, the Empress Isabella, despite his long absences from her. He was anxious that Philip should grow up sharing his own moral and sexual probity. He emphasised to his bachelor son the importance of chastity before marriage, and within marriage he advised him that an over-active sex life might lead to premature death. Nevertheless, Charles did conceive two illegitimate children; Margaret, born in 1521 before his marriage, and Don John, born in 1546 when Charles was a widower. However, compared, for example, to his contemporaries, Francis I of France and Henry VIII of England, Charles' record was distinctly abstemious.

A final testimony to Charles' lifelong religious devoutness was his decision to abdicate all of his titles in the mid-1550s. There were several factors, both personal and political, which inclined him towards such a course of action, but a religious motivation was very important. He wished to retire from the cares of the world and to prepare himself for death and afterlife in solitude and contemplation. He therefore had a villa built for himself in the Castilian countryside, adjoining the monastery of San Jeronimo of Yuste. He retired there in 1557. From his household he could see the celebration of mass and hear the monastic choir in the neighbouring church. He spent long hours reading religious works and discussing spiritual matters with his personal confessor. He died on 21 September 1558, attended by monks reading psalms.

To what extent did the Emperor Charles V live up to the knightly ideals of chivalry that he absorbed in his Burgundian childhood? Although he was ascetic in his own personal and religious outlook, he encouraged courtly display and knightly pageantry in the style of his Burgundian boyhood. Of more historical importance, he sought to maintain a code of honour and justice befitting a chivalric knight. When the troublesome religious dissident, Martin Luther, was summoned before him at Worms in 1521, Charles felt duty-bound to honour his promise of safe conduct and allow Luther to depart in peace. When, in 1526, the King of France broke a solemn promise to Charles over the provisions of the Franco-Habsburg Treaty of Madrid, Charles was genuinely outraged. In an already outdated chivalric gesture, he demanded that the French king meet him in hand-to-hand combat. The King of France declined, but the challenge exemplifies Charles' conception of himself as an honourable and valiant knight. Despite the pressures of political life he tried to maintain a highminded code of honour and he despised princes who failed to match his ideals. His words, uttered in the 1550s when his political fortunes were plummeting, were far from hollow: In no event and for nothing in the world will I act against duty and conscience.

In Charles' youth the skills of the knightly tournament were esteemed for the purposes of recreation and display. In his adulthood they were put to more serious use. He was always anxious to prove himself as a gallant military leader, in the tradition of chivalric valour. On numerous occasions his ministers attempted to dissuade him from leading his armies in person, but usually to no avail. During his reign he led his troops against Muslim, German and French enemies. In battle he showed considerable personal courage, and even foolhardiness. When he led a campaign against the German Protestants in the 1540s he was held in high esteem by his soldiers. Evidence of this appears in one of their songs:

> The Emperor is a man of honour.
> He marches in the foremost rank
> On horse or on foot.
> Take heart, all ye bold *landsknechts* (footsoldiers)
> For the Emperor himself has said;
> 'We will not yield!'

After the ensuing victory over the German Protestants at the Battle of Mühlberg in 1547, the great Italian painter, Titian, painted the Emperor in the pose of a conquering knight (see front cover). Therefore Charles continued to see himself in the knight-errant tradition of Burgundian chivalry and coveted the glory that went with bravery and leadership in battle.

However, a portrayal of Charles as a model of knightly virtue does not represent the whole picture. In some ways he was distinctly ill-suited for such a role. In his youth he had been most unprepossessing in facial appearance and bodily physique. As an adult the impression he made did not greatly improve. Contemporaries noted his bulging eyes, his large nose, his out-sized lower jaw (only thinly disguised by a beard) and his slight build (see pages 5 and 18). To make matters worse, he was plagued by all manner of ailments and diseases. He suffered from indigestion, asthma, piles and probably from diabetes. However, it was gout that most frequently incapacitated him. The disease arose from an excess of uric acid in the blood and caused painful swellings in the joints. He was first struck by it in his late twenties and for the rest of his life he was a regular sufferer. It frequently confined him to bed, his whole body racked with swellings and by his fifties he was very much a cripple. Therefore, observers were often struck by the frailty and infirmity of the Emperor. In 1546, for example, an Englishman commented, 'If he live two years, hang me on the third.' A year later, when Titian painted his celebrated work, his subject could, in reality, hardly sit on his horse because of gout. To this extent, then, Charles' image of knightly prowess is rather more myth than reality.

The Emperor's ill-health was greatly aggravated by a vice which fitted ill with both his knightly image and his Christian self-denial. Charles was an inveterate glutton. He started his day at 5am with a large breakfast and great quantities of iced beer. He ate and drank prodigiously for the rest of the day. He even received a special dispensation to forego fasting before partaking of communion. His family, physicians and confessors could do nothing to restrain his appetite. Even in his gout-ridden retirement his excesses continued. His chamberlain at Yuste reflected, 'Surely kings must think that their stomachs are not made like other men's.'

Finally, did Charles' schooling in affairs of state, so assiduously supervised by Chièvres, produce the conscientious and dutiful ruler that his dynasty and his subjects so desired? Here evidence is conflicting. Some historians have been impressed by the application he gave to state business. He liked to have political dispatches read to him personally and his precise and relevant written replies can be found in historical archives. Similarly, he received written advice (*consulta*) from his councils and the careful attention he gave to them is recorded in his written annotations to them. Some contemporaries were likewise complimentary about the Emperor's sense of duty. For example, a Venetian ambassador observed that he 'rejoices in consultations with and visits to his councils, which he attends diligently and where he spends most of his time'. However, there are also indications that he showed some slackness in the attention he gave to the routine government of his realms. He was, according to this evidence, prone to spells of laziness and to a preference for the more trivial pursuits of court life, particularly hunting. His confessor, for example, advised him:

> In your royal person indolence is at war with fame. I pray that God's grace will be on you . . . and that you will be able to overcome your natural enemies, good living and waste of time.

In addition, there is no doubt that Charles' ill-health, particularly his attacks of gout, often distracted him from attending to affairs of state. Furthermore, as he grew older he suffered from fits of depression during which ministers were frustrated by his inattention to state business. Sometimes he would amuse himself by aimlessly dismantling clocks and watches and then reassembling them. In the 1550s he suffered a series of mental breakdowns, during which he isolated himself from his ministers. According to one observer in 1553, 'he spent long hours sunk in thought and then wept like a child'.

3 Charles' Aims and Ambitions

Before proceeding to examine Charles V's career in the following chapters, it will be helpful to give some thought to his broader aims and ambitions. There is substantial agreement amongst historians as to the guiding principles which helped shape the Emperor's actions throughout his life. These can be divided into three areas, around which the three major chapters of this book are organised; Charles the Ruler, the Dynast and the Defender of the Faith. However, it should be borne in mind that these aims often overlapped and intermingled, and that it is highly unlikely that the Emperor would himself have recognised such a clear demarcation of his aims and objectives. Also historians are certainly not in complete agreement as to the relative importance that Charles attached to each of these aims and it is not necessarily the case that his order of priorities remained constant throughout his career.

How, then, do historians view the substance of Charles' aims and purposes? As a ruler, Charles' aims are usually considered to be somewhat conservative; he wished to preserve the existing order of things and to ensure continuity with the past. As one biographer has observed, he 'preferred that which had stood the test of time'. His greatest fear was of destabilising change within his dominions and of disruptive attack from without. His conception of his empire as a whole was also conservative. He had no blueprint for incorporating his individual dominions into a new and centralised political structure. Instead, he tended to regard his empire as a federation of independent territories united only in their common loyalty to his person and to the House of Habsburg. (In this book the word 'empire' is used to describe all of Charles' dominions. The word 'Empire' refers only to the Holy Roman Empire, or Germany.) As a dynast, Charles' ambitions are usually seen to have been more positive. He wished to protect and extend the fortunes of his family and to ensure the future greatness of the House of Habsburg. The biographer Karl Brandi argues that it was this dynastic principle that provided 'an inner unity' to the multi-faceted career of the Emperor. As a defender of the faith, Charles felt that he had been chosen by God to defend the Church and Catholic teachings. Such a role, he assumed, was incumbent upon him because he was both the pre-eminent prince in Christendom and Holy Roman Emperor. He saw the Pope as the spiritual leader of Christendom and himself as its secular and political leader. The obligations of such leadership were twofold. Firstly, he must attempt to bring peace to Christendom and maintain an undivided and universal faith. Secondly, he dreamt of leading Christendom in a crusade against the 'infidel' forces of Islam. His determination to revive the medieval spirit of the Crusades has been widely noted by historians.

Making Notes on 'Introduction to the Reign of Charles V'

This chapter is intended to provide background material for the more detailed chapters that follow. You should, therefore, take brief notes.
Charles' Inheritance
Read this section in conjunction with Charles' family tree (page 49). It is important to understand how he inherited his various realms. A good way to ensure that you have absorbed this information is to practise

Charles' upbringing and character

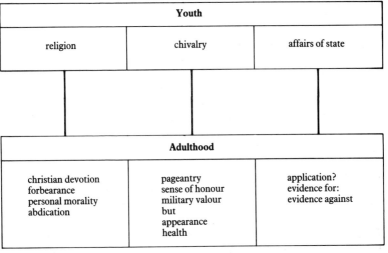

Youth		
religion	chivalry	affairs of state

Adulthood		
christian devotion forbearance personal morality abdication	pageantry sense of honour military valour but appearance health	application? evidence for: evidence against

Charles' aims and ambitions

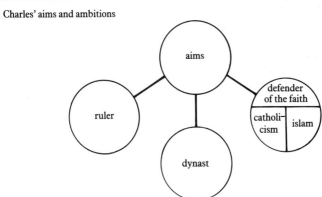

Summary – Introduction to the Reign of Charles V

writing out the family tree from memory, reminding yourself of what Charles inherited through each branch of the family.

Charles' Upbringing and Character

Answer the following questions in short paragraphs, and in your own words. For each one look at the earlier part of Section 2 which deals with Charles' youth and at the next part which assesses the extent to which his early experiences stamped his character and outlook for the rest of his life.

1. How important was religion to Charles V and what effect did it have on his outlook and personality?

2. What was chivalry and what effect did it have on his outlook and personality?
3. To what extent did he fit the ideal of the chivalrous knight?
4. How conscientious was Charles as a ruler?

Charles' aims and ambitions

In your own words, summarise Charles' aims and ambitions as identified in this chapter.

Source-based questions on 'Introduction to the Reign of Charles V'

Study the portraits of Charles on pages 5 and 18. Answer the following questions.

a) In what ways does the portrait on page 18 confirm what you have read about Charles' appearance and personality? *(3 marks)*
b) What techniques does the artist of the portrait on page 5 employ to give a different impression of Charles than that given on page 18. Answer in as much detail as possible. *(5 marks)*
c) Do you think the two artists had different motives in producing their portraits? Explain your answer. *(2 marks)*
d) What are the benefits and limitations of such portraits as historical evidence? *(5 marks)*

Studying Charles V

Studying Charles V is quite a challenging endeavour, given the extent and variety of his dominions and responsibilities. However, there are distinct benefits. His reign touches on so many aspects of European history in the first half of the sixteenth century that to study Charles is, in many ways, to study the political history of Europe as a whole during this period. If he is looked at early on in your course of study your efforts will be rewarded when you proceed to other topics and find that you already have much relevant knowledge at your disposal. If he is studied later on in your course you will find that you are already familiar with his impact on several areas of European history. For example, there is obviously a major overlap between Charles V and the Habsburg-Valois wars, the Ottoman Empire, the German Reformation and Early Modern Spain.

This overlap does provide some problems for examiners when they come to set examination questions. They must be careful not to ask candidates to write about aspects of Charles' career and provide them with the opportunity to use the same material in answering another question. From the student's point of view, it is fair to say that questions on Charles V can be unpredictable. Because of the range of the emperor's activities examiners have plenty of scope in selecting their questions. They may choose general questions which test your knowledge and understanding of his reign as a whole, or they may select narrower questions which demand a more detailed knowledge of a particular aspect of his career. Compare the following two questions:

1. To what extent were Charles V's problems of his own making?
2. How successfully did Charles overcome opposition to him in Spain?

Examiners also ask students to compare and contrast different aspects of Charles' reign. For example:

3. To what extent did Charles succeed as King of Spain and fail as Holy Roman Emperor?

Such a question is obviously less general than the first question quoted above, but less narrow than the second. Your material would have to be adapted accordingly.

Examiners also sometimes combine Charles V with his predecessors or successors in the same question. For example:

4. How successful were the Emperors Maximilian I and Charles V in asserting Imperial authority in Germany?
5. Compare Charles V and Philip II as rulers of Spain.

Again, a particular aspect of Charles' reign would occupy roughly half of your essay. The important lesson to be drawn from the above examples is that students must be highly flexible in preparing to answer examination questions on Charles V. It is important to be able to organise and arrange your material to enable your to answer questions that range from the broad overview to the narrower analysis of a particular aspect of the Emperor's reign.

CHAPTER 2

Charles the Ruler

1 The Burgundian Lands

a) The Political Background

The political life of the Burgundian lands was complex. The lands were ruled by the hereditary Duke of Burgundy, but the traditional lands of the dukes, Burgundy itself, had been lost to the French crown. The dukes' remaining lands formed a loose confederation of territories between France and the Holy Roman Empire (see map, page 15). They comprised Franche Comté, Luxembourg and the Netherlands. The latter formed the greater part of the Burgundian lands, and its provinces were often collectively known by this name. To the north lay territories like Friesland and Gelderland, which retained their independence. Most of the Burgundian lands were nominally still part of the Holy Roman Empire although parts of the Netherlands owed feudal obligations to France.

The political and administrative framework that Charles inherited in the Netherlands reflected the fragmented nature of the lands. The most powerful institutions were not those of the duke's central government but those of the many provinces (17 by 1543) which made up the Netherlands. These provinces had long prided themselves on their separate laws, privileges and institutions and attempted to safeguard their interests through their own provincial Estates (assemblies). The Estates represented their most powerful economic and political groupings. Given the wide dissimilarities between the provinces, it was not surprising that they found it difficult to come to mutual agreements on issues that affected the Netherlands as a whole. This was apparent at the proceedings of the Estates General, a representative assembly which brought together delegates from all the provinces of the Netherlands. Delegates used the Estates General to frustrate government policies which threatened the independence of the provinces or which attempted to impose a greater degree of unity upon the government of the Netherlands.

Charles' success in governing the Burgundian lands depended on his ability to secure the support of the two most important social groupings in his lands – the nobility and the town oligarchies. It was, above all, the nobility who monopolised political office. They held the most important posts at both local and provincial levels. It was, therefore, the nobility who most jealously guarded the privileges and independence of the provinces. However, local loyalties were often tempered by the prospect of advancement in Charles' court or administration, or

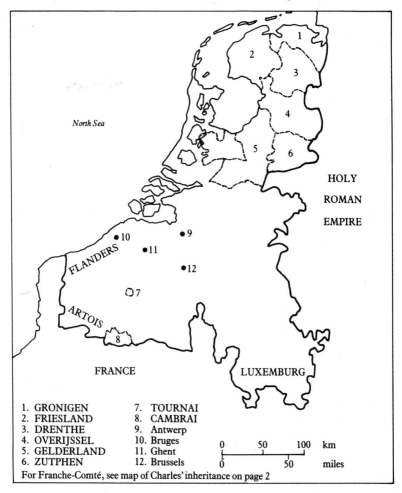

North Sea

HOLY

ROMAN

EMPIRE

FLANDERS

•10   •9

•11

•12

ARTOIS

◖7

8

FRANCE   LUXEMBURG

1. GRONIGEN   7. TOURNAI
2. FRIESLAND   8. CAMBRAI
3. DRENTHE   9. Antwerp
4. OVERIJSSEL   10. Bruges
5. GELDERLAND   11. Ghent
6. ZUTPHEN   12. Brussels

0   50   100   km

0   50   miles

For Franche-Comté, see map of Charles' inheritance on page 2

The Burgundian Lands

even by feelings of obligation and loyalty towards the hereditary duke.
Charles also had to take into account the ruling elites of the towns and
cities. Wealthy merchant and commercial families dominated politics in
the prosperous and largely self-governing towns and cities which made
the Netherlands one of the most highly urbanised regions of Europe.
They posed a further obstacle to centralised ducal control, and in the
provincial Estates they proved to be stout defenders of the interests of
their own towns and cities. They were particularly reluctant to divert
money from commerce and trade to Charles' imperial coffers.

b) Charles' Government of the Netherlands

Charles attached great importance to the good government of his Burgundian inheritance. The Netherlands were important to him, firstly, because his emotional and family ties were strong. This was the land of his birth and of his boyhood, and as he grew up he was encouraged to read the chronicles of the land's history and to revere the deeds of his paternal forbears. Secondly, the Netherlands were rich, and thus a fruitful source of revenue for his empire. As a Venetian observer commented, the Netherlands were 'the treasures of the king of Spain – these his mines, these his Indies, which have sustained all the emperor's enterprises'.

Yet Charles was largely an absentee ruler, despite his personal commitment to the Netherlands. He spent only 12 years there between 1516, when he acquired his wider empire, and his abdication in 1555. After the death of his most important Burgundian adviser, Guillaume de Croy Lord of Chièvres, in 1521 effective control of the Netherlands was given in Charles' absence to his aunt, Margaret of Austria, who had been regent, in name at least, since 1509. When Margaret died in 1530, Charles appointed his sister, Mary of Hungary, as Governess-General. Historians have given both Margaret and Mary an excellent press. Both were tough and astute politicians who appear to have done their best to promote the interests of the Netherlands. Mary, in particular, displayed an intelligent determination to protect her domains. During Charles' interminable wars with France she recognised the economic damage that was being inflicted upon the Netherlands and constantly worked and argued for peace. During times of crisis Mary would be in regular contact with Charles, both by letter and via personal ambassadors, but she was generally left to solve problems for herself. In 1543 she pleaded with Charles to return to the Netherlands immediately. Charles replied that he was content to trust in her judgement.

However, it should be noted that Charles maintained ultimate control over political developments in the Netherlands. This was most obviously the case in times of political emergency. For example, when the city of Brussels mutinied in 1528 it was Charles who immediately ordered the severe punishment of the rebels. In addition, Charles' authority was particularly clear-cut in the determination of the external affairs of the Netherlands. He decided upon matters of war and peace himself, and in 1536 turned a deaf ear to Mary's pleas that the Netherlands should be kept out of the war with France. Charles secured further control of events in the Netherlands by supervising the apparatus of government which existed to advise the governor and to implement policy. Indeed, when Mary was appointed in 1531 she was ordered by Charles to discard her current advisers, whom Charles suspected of being tainted by Protestant heresy. To provide further checks upon the actions of his governors Charles appointed advisory bodies. In the 1520s Margaret was supported by a council of state, largely made up of nobles, and by a financial advisory board. However, Charles became dissatisfied with this arrangement. In the early 1530s, when his attention returned to the running of his Burgundian lands, he reorganised the machinery of central government. He aimed both to strengthen central authority in the Netherlands and to limit the freedom of action of his governor. A strengthened council of state was given the power to meet without being convened by the duke's governor. The council was to be supported by new councils of finance and justice. These were to put the administration of finance and law under more centralised and bureaucratic control.

c) Charles' Successes

There has been an inclination on the part of historians to highlight the problems and difficulties which Charles experienced in this part of his empire. In some cases this has been based upon a careful examination of the historical evidence of Charles' reign, but it also arises from the fact that Charles' Burgundian lands were plunged into a prolonged period of crisis under his successor, Philip II, which ultimately was to rend the country in two. Employing historical hindsight, historians have naturally looked for the seeds of this calamity in the reign of Charles V. However, some historians have been inclined to a more sympathetic view. They have contrasted the firm maintenance of ducal authority and political order that the Netherlands experienced under Charles V with their violent and irretrievable collapse under Philip II from the 1560s onwards.

Charles successfully pursued a policy of geographical expansion and consolidation. He acquired Tournai in 1521 and Cambrai in 1543 as a result of success in wars against France (see map, page 15). By a combination of political intrigue and military conquest he extended his sovereignty northwards, over the provinces of Friesland (1523), ·
Utrecht and Overjssel (1528), Drenthe and Gronigen (1536) and Zutphen and Guelderland (1543). In 1548 Charles decided to impose a greater degree of unity over the lands he had inherited and acquired. This led him to look more closely at the contradictory position of the Burgundian lands within his empire. Thus, in the same year, they were formally reorganised into a single political unit, separate from the Holy Roman Empire. This was accomplished through negotiations with the German princes and through the subsequent provisions of the Augsburg Transaction. In 1549 he negotiated the Pragmatic Sanction which ensured that his heirs would inherit all 17 provinces. Although some historians view these initiatives as the official recognition of the existing political reality, others argue that they mark the real beginnings of the Netherlands as an independent political state.

Under Charles V there is little evidence of the serious levels of

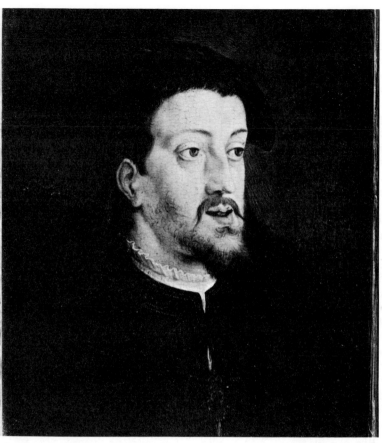

Anonymous portrait of Charles V

political discontent amongst the most powerful groups in the Netherlands that was to plague Philip II from the early years of his reign. The
nobles were given little cause to question or challenge Charles' ducal
authority. He made no direct attack upon their privileges or vested
interests and he used his extensive powers of patronage to win their
support. The nobility dominated the most powerful organ of central
government, the council of state. At court the leading nobles were
admitted to the prestigious Order of the Golden Fleece. This order
upheld the values of Christianity and medieval chivalry, but in politics
it also spoke authoritatively on behalf of the aristocracy of the
Netherlands. Charles made no attempt to undermine the independence
of the provinces and the nobility retained their monopoly over the office
of *Stadholder* (provincial governor). However, Charles was more reluc-

tant to accept the traditional rights and privileges of the towns and cities. Steps were taken to limit their rights to self-government. The authority of Charles' chief officials in the towns (bailiffs) was extended, to the detriment of locally elected representatives. The political independence of the towns was further undermined when the task of acting against heresy was transferred from the towns to provincial councils and to the centralised Inquisition. Nevertheless, Charles was cautious about interfering in the long-standing local rights of the towns and cities and he was anxious to maintain the loyalty of their ruling elites. He therefore chose the occasion for his attacks on urban independence with care. Tournai, Brussels and Ghent lost significant rights of self-government in 1522, 1528 and 1540 respectively, but only after rebelling against ducal authority. In addition, Charles concentrated much of his attention upon limiting the rights of the poorer classes within the government of the towns. In the case of Tournai, Brussels and Ghent he excluded the associations of the artisans and craftsmen, the guilds, from city government. Therefore, it can be argued that Charles was selective and cautious in his attacks upon the traditions of democratic self-government in the towns. The towns, in return, never showed signs of forming themselves into a political opposition to him, as the Castilian towns did in the early years of his rule in Spain (see page 24).

Some historians argue that Charles also enjoyed success in dealing with the religious affairs of the Netherlands. He considered his inability to stem the tide of Protestantism in Germany to be one of his greatest failures. Here, his weak political position encouraged him to make compromises with the Protestants. On the other hand, in the Netherlands he set himself up as the implacable scourge of heresy. 'What is tolerated in Germany' he wrote to his sister Mary, 'must never be suffered in the Netherlands.' Charles was fortunate in the Netherlands to receive substantial support from his most powerful subjects for the suppression of heresy. Their support was readily given because the Netherlands proved to be particularly receptive to radical strains of Protestantism, such as Anabaptism. Such religious beliefs appealed to the poor and the disadvantaged and easily became mixed up with ideas hostile to the privileges of the rich and to the existing social order. Charles was therefore able to set up instruments of centralised persecution without serious opposition from his leading subjects. The Inquisition was established in 1522, and in 1525 a series of extremely severe edicts, known as 'placards', were issued prohibiting Protestant ideas. In the latter stages of his reign Charles remained fearful of the spread of Protestant ideas, and in 1550 he introduced the death penalty for all religious heresy. In this harsh climate of repression the Netherlands were effectively sealed off from the new religious ideas. Anabaptism was reduced to a tiny underground movement after severe persecution in the 1530s and 1540s. In the Netherlands, then, religious heresy had no opportunity to coalesce into a broader movement of political dissent, as it did in Germany.

d) Charles' Failures

Such successful features of Charles' rule in the Netherlands must, however, be balanced against some of the more negative aspects of his reign. Historians agree, on the whole, that among all sections of Netherlands society the deepest and most widespread resentment was felt against Charles' financial exploitation of his Burgundian lands. His ceaseless financial demands were made in order to cover the defence of the Netherlands against France, but they were also necessitated by his many commitments outside of the Netherlands. In times of pressing need Charles demanded enormous sums from the Estates General of the Netherlands. His demand in 1537 for 200,000 guelders a month provoked widespread displeasure in addition to the open rebellion of the town of Ghent. Charles also demanded longer-term financial commitments from his subjects. In the 1549 Pragmatic Sanction Charles succeeded in securing from his Burgundian lands a commitment that they would contribute to the defence of the Holy Roman Empire by supplying twice the troops and money given by a German Elector, and three times as much should the Holy Roman Empire be threatened by the Ottoman Empire. During his last years Charles further increased the burden on the Netherlands to finance his Italian campaigns. This coincided with rising prices and the decline of the cloth industry in the Netherlands. The result was severe economic difficulties for many of his subjects. Such developments have led some historians to conclude that the Netherlands were ripe for revolt before Charles' abdication and the accession of Philip II.

Charles met with very little success in bringing the towns and cities of the Netherlands under more centralised control. His efforts to weaken their political independence were, as we have seen, very limited. The towns constantly complained about his financial exactions. They resisted Charles' efforts to allow delegates to the Estates General to act more independently of those whom they represented. The nobility similarly exhibited a sullen unwillingness to support some of Charles' demands. They protested regularly at both his financial requisitions and the incompetence of his administration. Such grievances were aired by the nobility with some monotony at meetings of the Order of the Golden Fleece. It has been noted that no coherent opposition to Charles' rule emerged from amongst the nobility, but there is some evidence that the disloyalty of the nobility to Philip II was foreshadowed in the reign of his father. Mary wrote to Charles in 1542 complaining bitterly that she was receiving practically no support from the Burgundian nobility for the government of the Duchy. In June 1554 Charles wrote to his son Philip warning him that an aristocratic opposition to his succession and to the continuation of the link between the Netherlands and Spain was emerging. There is additional evidence that suggests that this dissatisfaction amongst some of the most powerful nobles was paralleled by an increasing disaffection amongst the lesser nobility. They viewed the privileges of the higher nobility with envy, felt excluded from their fair share of ducal patronage and were suffering from economic difficulties themselves. It was this group that was to play a central role in the revolts against Philip II. Thus important political groups appeared to be moving against Habsburg rule in the Netherlands.

This was compounded, according to some historians, by Charles' failure to come to terms with the fundamental political problem of administering the Netherlands – the weakness of central authority in the face of provincial independence. The government of the Netherlands thus remained slow, cumbersome and difficult, as the Estates General consistently upheld provincial customs and interests and insisted both upon the redress of their grievances before the discussion of taxes and upon reporting back to the towns and provinces before attempting to formulate common policies. It can be argued that the turning-point came for Charles in 1534 when he proposed that the provinces should be brought into closer union in order to provide for the defence of the Netherlands as a whole. The Estates General rejected this attempt to impose a collective military and fiscal obligation on the Netherlands. After this Charles abandoned any hope of achieving a more unified political system in the Netherlands.

Criticisms have also been made of Charles' religious policies in the Netherlands. As we have seen, his determined persecution of heresy was largely successful in its immediate effects, but some historians have argued that Charles' repressive responses merely strengthened the tenacity of the remaining Protestants and drove them into more secretive and extreme channels. It has also been argued that they contributed to the wider process of disaffection with Charles' rule. The Netherlands, the homeland of Erasmus, the great advocate of religious toleration, and a land of pragmatic and self-satisfied merchants, viewed with distaste the disruptive excesses of Charles' religious persecution. Indeed, by the 1550s it became apparent that political leaders in the provinces were in many cases failing to implement Charles' heresy laws.

2 The Spanish Lands

a) The Political Background

In succeeding to the thrones of Spain, Charles inherited lands not dissimilar to the Netherlands in their disunity and complexity. Spain was a confederation of kingdoms comprising the crowns of Aragon and

Castile. The crown of Aragon was itself made up of the separate kingdoms of Catalonia, Valencia and Aragon (see map, page 23). Aragon also possessed the old empire of the Balearic islands, Sardinia, Sicily and Naples (see map, page 2), whilst through Castile Charles was to inherit the New World in the Americas. The union of Castile and Aragon achieved by Charles' predecessors was a personal union and not one based upon political and administrative unification. Each of these historic lands maintained its own customs and institutions. Indeed, there were still important sections of opinion in each which would happily have embraced a return to their old independence. As in the Netherlands, the towns of Castile were politically very important and enjoyed substantial rights of self-government and, in conjunction with the local nobility, dominated the *Cortes*, or parliamentary assembly, of Castile. In Aragon, on the other hand, the nobility wielded immense power on their own. For example, their ancient political liberties enabled them to dispense justice without reference to central government, and in Catalonia even to wage war independently. Such political power was carefully preserved by the Aragonese nobility. To this end the *Cortes* of Aragon developed as an extremely independent body. It insisted that the king redress their grievances before they would grant money to the crown. In Castile the authority of the crown was also weak when Charles came to the throne. Charles' predecessors had attempted to curb the powers of the nobility. They had also attempted to impose royal authority over the towns by the employment of royal agents (*corregidores*). However, in the early sixteenth century such successes as had been achieved looked increasingly under threat. With the death of Ferdinand of Aragon in 1516, royal authority, as exercised through the old and dying regent, Cardinal Cisneros, all but collapsed. When he attempted to establish a militia in order to secure public order, the Castilian towns and the nobility sabotaged the effort. It was against such a troubled backdrop that Charles arrived in Castile in 1517 to take up his crown.

b) Spain in Revolt, 1516–22

The period from 1516 to 1522 is commonly identified by historians as a critical period in the reign of the Emperor Charles V as King Charles I of Spain. A knowledge of the major developments during this period is thus crucial to an understanding of how Charles established his authority as King of Spain and, also, to the whole history of his reign. Charles was proclaimed joint ruler of Castile and Aragon with his mother, shortly after the death of Ferdinand of Aragon in January 1516. Charles' Burgundian advisers had moved quickly, as legally his mother was still the sole and legitimate heir. In September 1517 Charles arrived in Spain and secured from her the right to act as king. Charles and his advisers proceeded to assume control over the government of

1. Corunna
2. Santiago
3. Pamplona
4. Villalar
5. Valladolid
6. Madrid
7. Toledo
8. Yuste
9. Barcelona
10. Lisbon
11. Seville
12. CERDAGNE
13. ROUSSILON

The Kingdoms of Aragon

0   100   200 km
0   50   100 miles

Spain in the early sixteenth century

Spain without reference to Joanna, justifying their actions because of her periodic fits of madness. Charles' next task was to extract from the *Cortes* of his kingdoms their acceptance of his claim to the crowns. The *Cortes* of both Castile and Aragon agreed to this, voting Charles a *servicio* (a sum of money to be raised through taxation), but only after making plain their doubts about the new king and their determination not to be taken advantage of by him. 'Most powerful lord, you are in our service' the *Cortes* of Castile advised Charles, whilst the *Cortes* of Aragon received him with even greater rudeness.

In January 1519 Emperor Maximilian died. Charles and his advisers determined to secure the succession. To meet the additional financial burden that this bid would entail, Charles' personal adviser, Chièvres, summoned the Castilian *Cortes* to Santiago, a remote location suitable only for the departing Charles and his retinue. Despite the fact that the previous *servicio* had not yet expired, it was obvious to all concerned that the purpose behind this summons was the need for a further grant of money. Thus the deliberations of the *Cortes* at Santiago (and later at Charles' point of departure, Corunna) were stormy and another *servicio* was only voted very narrowly after considerable persuasion and pressure had been brought to bear by the crown. To make matters worse, on leaving Spain in May 1520, Charles added insult to injury by breaching earlier promises about the employment of foreigners. He appointed his Burgundian tutor, Adrian of Utrecht, as regent in his absence.

Charles and his advisers had antagonised his subjects to such an extent that in June 1520 a major revolt broke out in Castile. The revolt was known as the revolt of the *Communeros*. The majority of the towns of Castile, led by Toledo, joined together in a league (*communeros*) to resist the imposition of Habsburg authority. The revolt was headed by what was in effect a revolutionary government. The towns overthrew royal authority where they could, refused to pay taxes and expelled royal officials. At first the nobility (and indeed the clergy) did nothing to help their new king. However, as the revolt developed, its leadership became increasingly riven by argument and factionalism, and its social and political programme, under different leaders, became increasingly radical and extreme. The Castilian nobility, fearing assaults upon their own properties and privileges, went over to the side of royal authority and decisively defeated the rebels at the Battle of Villalar in April 1521.

Meanwhile a separate revolt had started in late 1519 in Valencia and it was not suppressed until the summer of 1522. For the historian of Charles' rule in Spain it can be argued that this revolt was of far less importance. Its origins lay in the distinctive racial, social and political circumstances of Valencia and historians are agreed that the revolt arose less from a conflict between the crown and its subjects than from conflict between the workers in the towns and the nobility. The *Germania* revolt was so-called from the armed brotherhoods, *Germania*, into which the rebels organised themselves. However, it did attract widespread support, and for a substantial period of time controlled most of the kingdom of Valencia. Like the *Communeros* revolt, it was also finally put down by a nobility fearful of the threat to their own interests. Thus, when Charles returned to Spain in July 1522, the land was largely pacified and his position was considerably more secure than it had been in 1520 when he had left. The extent to which Charles and his circle bear the responsibility for precipitating such an early political crisis in Spain, and the extent to which they were successful in dealing with their early difficulties must now be assessed.

Charles certainly did not cut much of a figure when he arrived in Spain as a rather sullen and insecure 17-year-old looking, according to J. H. Elliot, 'like an idiot' and apparently dominated by his advisers. He spoke no Spanish and was totally ignorant of Spain and Spanish affairs. In addition to Charles' personal failings, there were other reasons why the Spanish were lukewarm towards him. Charles was not the desired heir of the majority of his subjects. They would have preferred Charles' younger brother, Ferdinand, a Spaniard by upbringing who had been the favourite of Ferdinand of Aragon. It was in many ways a wise move to send Ferdinand out of the country in May 1517, but this was taken as an insult by many Spaniards. The presence in Spain of Charles' mother further compounded his difficulty in winning acceptance. The Aragonese, in particular, were reluctant to acknowledge Charles as king while his mother lived. Charles' decision to contest the Imperial election further aggravated the situation. Spaniards naturally feared the consequences of having an absentee king and suspected that Spanish interests would be sacrificed to those of the Holy Roman Empire.

Against such a background, Charles' position in Spain was clearly precarious, but historians tend to highlight the role of Charles' Burgundian advisers as the decisive factor in provoking actual resistance. However, there is some dispute over the extent of their provocation and this derives, in part, from the propaganda and counter-propaganda of the time. Some historians, like Henry Kamen, accuse Charles' circle of behaving 'as though they were in a conquered country', whilst others suggest that such allegations are exaggerated. Nevertheless, the Burgundians around Charles certainly saw it as legitimate to further their own interests and that of their friends and this involved acquiring Spanish property, wealth, honours and public appointments. Charles appeared to many to be in the hands of an unscrupulous and self-seeking foreign clique. His principal adviser, Chièvres, appointed his own nephew to the prestigious position of Archbishop of Toledo on the death of Cardinal Cisneros, and, the appointment of the Dutch bishop, Adrian of Utrecht, as regent was for many the last straw.

The new monarch's actions in Spain certainly made political disloyalty and open rebellion more likely. Therefore, some interpretations of the period 1516 to 1522 stop here and attribute the political emergencies of the period solely to the crown's insensitive behaviour. Historians, such as Henry Kamen and J. H. Elliot, go somewhat further in their explanations. They focus upon the deep divisions within Spanish society and argue that the arrival of the Habsburg monarchy was not on its own sufficient to provoke the troubles of 1516–22. What it did was to trigger already existing and deep-rooted anxieties and divisions. For example, the Castilians deeply resented the fact that Charles had chosen to spend substantially longer in the kingdom of Aragon than in that of Castile, reflecting an old rivalry between Spain's two major kingdoms. Charles' arrival also tended to polarise different economic interest groups. Wool exporters in Spain welcomed the Netherlands connection and the opportunities of the Netherlands market, while textile producers feared increased competition from Netherlands imports. And some in-depth studies of the *Communeros* revolt have found that rapid social, economic and political change in Castile was making some sort of upheaval virtually inevitable. For example, in Stephen Haliczer's work it is argued that a wealthy and growing urban middle class in Castile was becoming increasingly resentful at the political dominance of the Castilian landed nobility. The fact that a succession of weak governments had favoured the nobility at the expense of the towns meant that the latter were already predisposed to a revolutionary course of action before the arrival of the new Habsburg king in 1517.

It is all the more remarkable, then, that by the end of 1522 the unrest had come to an end, and that for the rest of Charles' reign such difficulties never recurred. How was a peaceful end to the unrest achieved? The *Germania* revolt was put down by the nobility of Valencia and not by the crown. Nor can it be argued that the responsibility for putting down the Revolt of the *Communeros* was predominantly Charles'. He was not in Spain at the time. He tended to follow the advice of Adrian of Utrecht and of the two co-regents he appointed in the autumn of 1522. Indeed, one of his co-regents wrote to him in November as follows:

> I am astonished to see the little interest which your Highness vouchsafes to the interests of our kingdoms and their pacification; for neither in the shape of money, men or artillery has your majesty sent me any aid – no, not even in paper and ink.

At best Charles can be commended for accepting wise counsels, for the concessions and conciliatory gestures of the crown did much to undermine the momentum of the revolt. The collection of the *servicio* was suspended, the appointment of the two co-regents was widely welcomed, Charles promised not to appoint foreigners in the future, and the unpopular Chièvres was replaced by Mercurino Gattinara, the respected counsellor of Charles' mother. Charles' return to Spain with an army of foreign mercenaries and having made an effort to learn some Spanish also helped to strengthen his position.

c) The Government of Spain, 1522–56

Charles came to see Spain as the centre of his world empire. As early as 1523 he referred to his Spanish lands as 'The head of all the rest.' He spent more time in Spain (17 years) than he did in any other part of the empire. His stay from 1522–9 was the longest continuous period he spent in any of his dominions. It was not surprising when he chose Spain as the place of his retirement and burial. Such a commitment to Spain stemmed partly from the fact that it was an extremely important source of revenue for Charles. But, it also arose from a deep and genuine pride and affection that Charles developed towards his Spanish inheritance.

However, for most of the time Charles was unable to rule Spain in person and so, again, he relied upon members of his family to head his government. When he left Spain in 1529 he appointed his wife, the Empress Isabella, as regent. She governed with the help of the Archbishop of Toledo, Cardinal Tavera, until her death in 1539. Several leading ministers were then given control of Spain, most notably Tavera, the Duke of Alba and Francisco de los Cobos. In 1542 Charles appointed his teenage son, Philip, as regent. Charles' correspondence with Philip at the time indicates that he expected his new regent to rule in accordance with his own wishes:

1 To enable you the better to fulfil your part I have left you here in Spain all the members of my royal council and given special instructions to them, which I send to you with Cobos. I beseech you to act in accordance with what I tell you. The royal council
5 will see to the administration on Justice and will care for the welfare of the land. Support them in their endeavours. Do not permit the publication of interdicts and the prohibition of worship except on the most urgent grounds, or unless the commands proceed from the Holy See itself, when you must
10 religiously respect them, for in these times many men no longer respect the Holy See. Trust the Duke of Alba as commander-in-chief of the army, obey my instructions in your dealings with the Council of State, the Council for the Indies, for finance, for the Order of the Golden Fleece, and in your relations with the
15 Inquisition. Have a special care to finance which is today the most important department of state; the treasury has a clear knowledge of the means which are at your disposal. . . Every man needs advice, and so I ask you to make Don Juan de Zúñiga your watch and your alarum in all things. I too have commanded him to do
20 his own part therein and to speak sharply if he must. Sleep is often sweet and an alarum commonly a nuisance. Therefore remember that he acts only out of devotion and duty to me, and be grateful to him.

Philip remained regent until his accession to the throne in 1556, although during his short absences from Spain his place was taken by other members of the family. As in the Netherlands, Charles' regents were served by leading ministers and advisers, whom Charles himself selected. However, in Spain Charles was anxious that experienced ministers should not usurp the authority of his regents, and of his young son in particular. In 1543 he gave Philip some confidential advice on how to deal with some of his more powerful ministers:

1 Let me once again rehearse to you all that I said to you in Madrid,
concerning the personalities and private rivalries of those about
my court and in the government. Make it clear to everyone that
you hold yourself aloof from all parties and quarrels. In order to
5 emphasise your impartiality I have included the heads of both
parties in your ministry. This will prevent you from falling under
the influence of either or becoming the instrument of their feuds.
    The Cardinal of Toledo is a good man and in all serious
questions you can rely on his honesty. Only do not subject
10 yourself wholly to his influence, lest men should say, on account
of your youth, you were but a tool in his hand. The Duke of Alba
can be counted on to support whichever party best suits his
private interest; I have therefore excluded him, together with all
other grandees, from the inner circle of the government. He is
15 ambitious, bear himself with as much seeming humility as he
may. He will do his best to make himself agreeable to you,
probably with the help of feminine influence. Take heed of him,
therefore; yet trust him implicitly in all military matters.

During his long stay in Spain, 1522–9, Charles worked to overhaul
and improve the system of administration which supported his regents
and his chief ministers. This was done partly upon the promptings of
his most influential adviser in the 1520s, Mercurino Gattinara, who was
anxious to provide more centralised control over the empire as a whole.
In other ways, though, the reforms of the 1520s were very much a
continuation of the administrative reforms undertaken by Ferdinand
and Isabella in their reigns. Ferdinand and Isabella had developed a
system of 'conciliar government', whereby specialist committees, or
councils, supervised the administration of particular geographical areas
or of particular governmental functions. These councils had no fixed
base, but were obliged, where possible, to remain at the monarch's
side. They met regularly and gave the monarch written reports
(*consultas*) on their deliberations. Their role was advisory and the
monarch was at liberty to ignore their advice.
    From Ferdinand and Isabella Charles inherited the Council of
Castile. It acted as a court of law in hearing appeals but, more
importantly, it concerned itself with the administration of most of
Castile's internal affairs. Charles' role in modernising it was twofold; he
halved its size, in order to improve efficiency, and increased the
representation of men of proven administrative efficiency whilst dimi-
nishing the representation of the Castilian aristocracy.
    Charles also inherited the Council of Aragon. Its duties were similar
to those of the Council of Castile, but its administrative role was more
limited. Charles, again, reduced the participation of the aristocracy.
However, he preserved the Council of Aragon's responsibility for the
Habsburg possessions in Italy. On the other hand, in the case of the

Americas a new council, the Council of the Indies, was formed in 1524. It was given powers well beyond those enjoyed by the councils responsible for Charles' European territories; it controlled all administrative, judicial and church matters relating to the Indies. Another new council established by Charles was the Council of State. In theory, its role was to advise the emperor on all matters of foreign and domestic policy and to oversee the work of the other councils. However, in practice, Charles and his regents largely dispensed with its advice. It did, nevertheless, provide Charles with a useful source of patronage; membership of the council conferred social prestige upon leading nobles, if little political power. An offshoot of the Council of State was the Council of War. It was set up in 1522 to meet the military requirements of the empire. It comprised the Council of State and a number of military experts. The last of the Councils set up under Charles was the Council of Finance. It was instituted by Gattinara in 1522. Although it remained a Castilian institution, with Castilian members, it soon came to supervise Charles' wider imperial income and expenditure. It developed a new system for the administration of finance in Castile and the empire. As such, it was the most innovative and important of the new councils.

The development of the conciliar system provided Charles with several advantages in the government of Spain. The Councils of Castile and Aragon were staffed by natives of these kingdoms and were thus useful in keeping Charles informed about the feelings of his subjects in these territories. Generally, the councils were valuable in checking that Charles' regents and ministers were following his instructions during his absences. Furthermore, in expanding the role of professional administrators at the expense of the nobility, Charles enhanced the efficiency and political neutrality of his administrative system. Yet, it would be a misleading exaggeration to suggest that Charles' conciliar system amounted to a modern style of bureaucratic government. Charles' councils were only a very early step in this direction and their powers remained limited. There was a considerable and confusing overlapping of functions between the various councils and their role remained advisory. It was such shortcomings in the conciliar system that gave rise to a new source of political power in Charles' Spain – the royal secretaries.

The political influence of Charles' secretaries expanded rapidly. It was they who supervised the proceedings of the various councils, preparing agendas and dealing with correspondence. It was they who provided the vital link between the king and the councils. One secretary in particular, Francisco de los Cobos, came to dominate Charles' administrative machinery. His rise to prominence accelerated rapidly after the death of Gattinara in 1530 and he soon acquired the position of secretary to most of Charles' councils. As such, he supervised all policy in relation to Castile, the Indies and Italy. Cobos accompanied Charles on all of his travels until 1539, when he returned to Spain and devoted himself to administering Spanish affairs. In Charles' absence he ruled Spain in conjunction with Charles' regents. His career highlights the fact that the conciliar system failed to function effectively until subordinated to the direction of powerful individuals who enjoyed the king's favour. In many ways it was the royal secretaries, and Cobos in particular, who dealt with the tasks which, in theory, belonged to the councils.

d) Charles' Successes

The period of Charles' reign from 1522–56 was remarkably tranquil after the turmoil of the years 1516–22. The absence of any serious social or political disorder has led some historians to conclude that it constitutes a distinct and successful period of Charles' rule in Spain. Indeed, one historian has observed that 'it almost seems as if for 20 or 30 years the country had no internal history.' The absence of social, political and religious conflict is striking in the context of the European history of the time. Historians and students of history often focus more upon dramatic upheaval and disturbance in the past and less upon stability and peace. However, a balanced assessment of Charles' reign as King of Spain must explore the origins of Spain's political stability after 1522 and Charles' contribution to it.

There are various reasons why Charles was able to overcome the initially unfavourable reactions of his subjects. He developed impressive regal qualities in manhood which evoked loyalty and affection amongst his peoples. There was no fixed royal capital during his residence in Spain. He travelled through his various Spanish territories in order to meet and listen to his subjects. His success in governing Aragon, some historians argue, is easier to explain than Castile. His interference in the traditional customs, laws and privileges of Aragon was minimal. He tolerated their largely independent political life in which a powerful native nobility dominated. The relative poverty of Aragon offered little incentive for Charles to intervene. However, it was in Castile that Charles' financial and manpower demands were at their most burdensome and relentless. How, then, did he succeed in maintaining such a secure, and some would argue popular, position here? His success owed much to his victory over the *Communeros* revolt. He was able to re-establish his authority over the towns by re-appointing his royal agents, the *corregidores*. He was seldom troubled by the Castilian *Cortes* after the *Communeros* revolt. Charles now dictated that delegates to the *Cortes* should attend with full powers of decision-making. Henceforth, he found the delegates more amenable to royal persuasion once they had left their towns and arrived at the *Cortes*. This authority over the Castilian *Cortes* can be contrasted to Charles' difficulties with the Estates General of the Netherlands, where delegates continually had to refer back to those who had sent them. In addition, in Castile Charles refused to allow the *Cortes* to make the granting of supplies to the crown dependent upon the redress of grievances. When the Castilian *Cortes* attempted to assert such a principle in 1523, Charles forced them to back down, confident of his position as recent victor over the towns of the *Communeros*. From this time on he was free to accept or reject the petitions of the Castilian *Cortes* at will. The obstacles posed by the towns to royal authority had, in effect, disappeared. The Castilian *Cortes* became little more than a tax-voting body. It met fifteen times during Charles' reign, usually when he returned to Spain in need of money. The *Cortes* invariably voted substantial subsidies to the crown. It can be argued, therefore, that an important factor in explaining Spain's political stability after 1522 was the triumph of royal authority over the Castilian towns and over the Castilian *Cortes*. This was, perhaps, the most important legacy of the *Communeros* revolt.

The Castilian nobility enjoyed substantial advantages under Charles. Their pride was flattered and their self-interest satisfied as Charles increasingly loosened his ties with his Burgundian lands and put Spain at the centre of his empire. Castilian nobles found lucrative employment in the running of Charles' empire. In addition, Charles exempted the nobility from the heaviest tax burdens. As a result, it has been argued that Charles' partnership with the Castilian nobility was one of the major pillars of his success in ruling Spain. During the *Communeros* revolt the nobility had proved their value to the crown in the maintenance of effective royal government. In its aftermath, Charles was careful to avoid offending them. But the victory of the nobility over the *Communeros* rebels brought them into a longer-term alliance with a monarchy much strengthened in its own right.

Stability in Spain depended also on the absence of religious division. Under Charles Spain preserved a unified church, committed to Catholic orthodoxy. The religious upheaval occasioned by the Protestant challenge in other parts of Europe hardly touched Spain. By 1558 there had been only 105 cases of Lutheranism tried in Spain, of which 66 involved foreigners. Even the ideas of moderate Catholic reformers, such as Erasmians, were suppressed from the 1530s onwards. Charles' maintenance of Catholic orthodoxy was greatly aided by the conservative religious instincts of the Church in Spain and of his Spanish subjects. However, Charles gave his personal approval to the suppression of new religious ideas. He supported the work of the Spanish Inquisition, a ruthless tribunal for the trying and punishment of religious heresy. In the last year of his life Charles personally ordered that Protestants uncovered at Valladolid and Seville be immediately put to death. Some historians have criticised Charles for fostering a narrow and rigid intellectual and religious life in Spain. However, he viewed with great pride his success in protecting the country from the contagion of religious heresy.

e) Charles' Weaknesses

That Spain enjoyed a remarkable period of political peace after 1522 is not in dispute, but some historians are cautious about reading too much into this. Charles was certainly successful at overawing and suppressing the overt, political resistance of the early years of his reign. However, this does not necessarily signify that grievances evaporated or that all hostility disappeared. It is difficult for historians to measure the attitudes and opinions of the Spanish people in an age before opinion polls and extensive written records. But it has been argued that the relative tranquility of the post-1522 period betokens less an enthusiastic acceptance of the Habsburg succession and more a resigned submission to Charles' superior force. There is some evidence of popular hostility to Charles. A Spanish commentator, writing during his reign, relates that whilst out hunting Charles met a Castilian peasant who failed to recognise him. Charles took the opportunity to ask which he thought were the best and the worst of the five Castilian kings he had lived under. He identified Charles as the worst and gave his reasons; he had left his wife for foreign lands, he had taken with him all the treasures of Spain and the New World and he was ruining the peasants with taxes.

The historian can also detect signs of unease and foreboding in the statements of those in positions of power and responsibility. Throughout Charles' reign the meetings of the Castilian *Cortes* urged Charles to reduce his financial impositions and return to Castile to attend to their problems. Similarly, it is clear that Charles' representatives in Spain grew increasingly alarmed at developments in the country. In the 1530s Empress Isabella repeatedly exhorted Charles to return to Castile and to address its problems. In the 1540s both Philip and Cobos urged Charles to recognise the grave difficulties facing Spain. For example, Philip wrote to Charles in 1543 describing the situation in Castile in the following terms:

1 With what they pay in other ordinary and extraordinary dues the
  common people, who have to pay these *servicios*, are reduced to
  such misery that many of them walk naked. And the misery is so
  universal that it is even greater among the vassals of nobles than it
5 is among Your Majesty's vassals, for they are unable to pay their
  rents, lacking the wherewithal, and the prisons are full.

Some historians have pointed out that the situation was not much better in Aragon. They argue that by ignoring the particular needs of Aragon, Charles allowed dangerous levels of resentment, faction-fighting and violence to build up. The result was a rebellion in Aragon during the first three years of the reign of Philip II. Therefore, an analysis of Charles' rule in Spain after 1522 would seem to suggest that, although he enjoyed success in containing active opposition, the contentment and loyalty of his subjects cannot be taken for granted.

As King of Spain, Charles has received most criticism from historians for his financial management of his Spanish inheritance. Spain bore the brunt of his vast imperial demands. In his own words, 'I cannot be sustained except by my realms in Spain.' In reality he meant Castile. Traditionally, the most important tax the crown raised from Castile had been the *alcabala*, a sales tax similar to the modern-day Value Added Tax. As such, it was payable by all classes of society. However, in 1534 Charles allowed it to be replaced by a local lump sum payment. Its yield subsequently fell as inflation reduced its value. As the amount derived from the *alcabala* fell, Charles became increasingly reliant upon the *servicio*, a sum raised by the Castilian *Cortes*. The *servicio* became, in effect, a regular tax and not, as it had been previously, a subsidy voted periodically by the *Cortes* to the crown. Charles' income from the *servicio* more than trebled, rising to 410,000 ducats in 1555. The nobility were exempt from this tax. In addition, Charles received substantial revenues from the Church in Spain and from his possessions in the Americas. From the latter he was the recipient of an average of 220,000 ducats per year, much of it in the form of silver bullion.

Despite exploiting such sources of revenue as fully as he could, they proved to be insufficient to his needs. The situation deteriorated from the 1530s onwards, as it became more difficult to increase revenues from other parts of the empire. Charles was forced to turn more and more to Castile. His first recourse was to borrowing. He raised interest-bearing loans (*juros*) from his subjects and guaranteed repayment from the crown's ordinary revenues. By 1556 the repayment of the *juros* consumed about 65 per cent of the crown's normal income. Further loans were obtained, at escalating interest rates, from international bankers. They were guaranteed on the security of the Castilian crown. Charles also sold public offices and certificates of nobility to augment his revenues. Against a background of such dire financial necessity, the tax exemptions of the Castilian nobility became increasingly anomalous. In 1538 Charles attempted to bring them into the regular system of taxation by introducing a new tax on food, the *sisa*. Like the *alcabala*, this was to be a tax on consumers, payable by all. A general *Cortes* was called at which the Castilian nobility, as well as the towns, were represented. The nobility refused to approve the new tax. Charles dropped the *sisa*, mindful of the value of a loyal nobility to the successful government of his kingdom.

For the remainder of his reign royal finances remained in acute difficulties. Charles was consistently spending more than he received in revenues and an increasing proportion of his revenues had to be used to finance his debts. In 1546 Cobos advised Charles to:

1 Remember the importance of finding a remedy for the relief of
these kingdoms, because of the extreme need, for otherwise there
could not fail to be serious trouble, because the need is so
notorious that not only are the natives of the kingdom aware of it
5 and are refusing to take part in any financial transaction, but even
foreigners . . . are doing the same thing, because they know there
is no source from which payments can be made.

On his accession in 1556, Philip II was forced to suspend all
payments from the Castilian treasury and to convert the crown's debts
into *juros*. Philip, and future Spanish monarchs, found it impossible to
shake off the legacy of debt inherited from the days of Charles.

Spain, and Castile in particular, paid a heavy price for Charles'
financial administration. His extensive borrowing did great damage to
the Spanish economy in the longer-term and fed price inflation. Foreign
financiers came to dominate important parts of the economy. Much
needed investment in trade and industry was hit, as businessmen opted
instead for the safe financial return guaranteed by the purchase of *juros*.
The failure to end the tax immunities of the nobility was equally
damaging as many Spaniards abandoned trade and industry in order to
buy noble status and the tax exemptions it conferred. Spanish society
became increasingly divided, as those most able to pay taxes contributed little, whilst the rest had to shoulder an ever-increasing tax
burden.

3 Germany

a) The Political Background

Charles inherited a large conglomeration of territories in central Europe
when his grandfather, the Holy Roman Emperor Maximilian I, died in
January 1519. He immediately inherited the Habsburg lands in Austria
and around the upper Rhine. However, by 1522 these had been handed
over to his brother Ferdinand with full hereditary rights. In June 1519
Charles succeeded Maximilian as Holy Roman Emperor. This title was
elective and not hereditary. Seven of Germany's leading princes
(electors) selected each new emperor by majority vote. The title had
been monopolised by the House of Habsburg since 1438, but Maximilian had failed to arrange for Charles' succession before he died.
Charles, therefore, had to submit himself to a vigorous and expensive
election campaign in order to secure the support of the German
electors. In this he was successful, fending off challenges from the king
of England and the king of France. The title he gained is misleading.
Indeed, in the eighteenth century a wit referred to the Holy Roman
Empire as being neither Holy, nor Roman, nor an Empire. In theory,

the Holy Roman Emperor was the secular head of the Christian world, who ruled Christendom in conjunction with its spiritual head, the Pope. In practice, the Holy Roman Emperor was the ruler of Germany. Germany itself was large and relatively densely populated; some 20 million inhabitants lived in an area of central Europe bordered by the Baltic in the north, and the Alps in the south, by France in the west and by Hungary and Poland in the east (see map, page 36).

The degree to which Spain and the Netherlands were divided and fragmented was as nothing compared with Germany. There were over 300 princely, ecclesiastical and urban states which conducted their affairs more or less independently of imperial jurisdiction. Germany was, in effect, a jigsaw of small and largely autonomous states and territories. Yet the title of Holy Roman Emperor was a highly-prized one. Considerable prestige attached to it because its holder could claim to represent all Christian peoples in secular matters. If the willing support of his German subjects was forthcoming, the Emperor could enjoy substantial military and financial resources. His subjects were proud of their German nationality, and there was a widespread feeling that a greater degree of unity in the Empire was desirable, even if there was little agreement on how this could be achieved. The Emperor set the agenda at meetings of the German Parliament (the Imperial Diet) and he negotiated with the Diet over its final decisions. In matters of law he was the supreme judge in Germany. His right to bestow titles and offices on his German subjects gave him further political influence. On the other hand, Germany possessed no effective institutions which provided for the government of the Empire as a whole. Although the Imperial Diet acted as a kind of national parliament, it only assembled irregularly and infrequently. The Emperor possessed no permanent imperial army, nor any established system of imperial taxation. However, it was in his relationship with the cities and the princes of the Empire that the weaknesses of the Emperor were most evident.

The powers and privileges of the German electors and other princes severely limited the Emperor's political authority in Germany. The powers of the princes had increased throughout the fifteenth century. Most controlled the administration of justice within their own lands. Some of the more powerful princes had begun to acquire the trappings and resources normally associated with the monarchies of the period. For example, they attracted the lesser nobility to their courts for employment. Maximilian I had recognised the weakness of imperial authority at the centre but, rather than attempting to remedy it, he had moved towards a system of government based on regional organisations. Germany was divided into ten Imperial Leagues. In each league the princes and the cities were given collective responsibility for law and order. The Swabian League was the best organised and the most successful, providing the mainstay of political order in the south of Germany. This system of leagues further reinforced the role of the

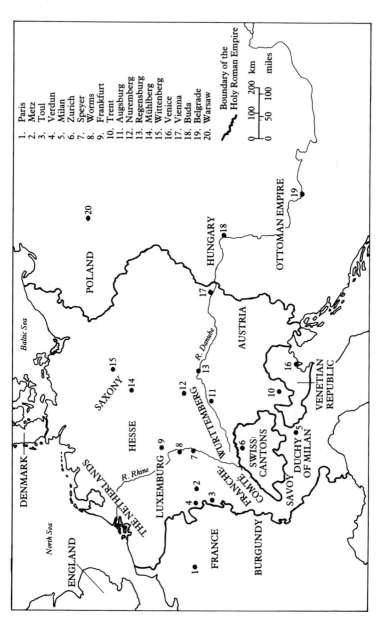

1. Paris
2. Metz
3. Toul
4. Verdun
5. Milan
6. Zurich
7. Speyer
8. Worms
9. Frankfurt
10. Trent
11. Augsburg
12. Nuremberg
13. Regensburg
14. Mühlberg
15. Wittenberg
16. Venice
17. Vienna
18. Buda
19. Belgrade
20. Warsaw

Boundary of the
Holy Roman Empire

The Holy Roman Empire

princes in the government of Germany. Nevertheless, some historians argue that Charles' position was not hopeless and that some form of compromise between imperial authority and princely autonomy was still possible.

In theory the Emperor enjoyed the allegiance of the Imperial Free Cities, of which there were about 80. However, their allegiance was largely nominal and they were accustomed to running their own affairs. Similarly, loyalty to the Emperor was traditionally expected of the imperial knights, a class of lesser nobility, but they too were proud of their independence. Moreover, their estates were much smaller than those of the German princes and they had suffered acute economic difficulties as the German agrarian economy faltered in the fifteenth century. Many had been forced into a state of dependency upon the princes or had taken to the countryside as bandits or highwaymen.

b) The Imperial Reform Movement

From the late 1400s the German princes began to work for a reform of the government of the Empire. They recognised that a more co-ordinated administration might enable them to protect their territorial interests collectively. They also saw the opportunity to extend their power by creating central institutions of government which they themselves could control. The first product of their efforts was Maximilian's reluctant establishment of an Imperial Chamber Court in 1495. This was to be the supreme legal authority throughout the Empire. However, the Emperor, fearing a diminution of his own authority, ignored its legal pre-eminence and the experiment made little progress. In 1500 Maximilian, in need of money and troops, agreed to set up a Regency Council. The council would allow the princes to rule Germany in the Emperor's absence and when he was resident it would act as a forum in which they could press their claims. However, the success of the princes was very short lived. Maximilian resented such a curtailment of his own role in government and put an end to the council in 1502. Nevertheless, the princes continued to press for the restoration of such a council. Historians have tended to emphasise the *dual* potential of this movement for imperial reform. It might certainly lay the foundations for the exclusion of the Emperor from the government of the Empire. It might, alternatively, provide the Emperor with centralised institutions of government of potential benefit to himself.

c) Charles' Government of Germany

In 1521, at a meeting of the Imperial Diet at Worms, Charles seemed to hold out the prospect of firm imperial leadership. 'It is not our mind and will to have many lords' he announced, 'but only one, as is the tradition of the sacred Empire.' However, he was absent from the

Empire between 1521 and 1530 and his deputy, his brother Ferdinand, had other territorial responsibilities and lacked the imperial dignity of the Emperor himself. Furthermore, it was evident from the very beginning of Charles' reign that the wishes of the German princes could not be ignored. Before he was promised the support of Germany's electoral princes in his bid to become Holy Roman Emperor, he had to sign a solemn undertaking, or 'capitulation'. In it he promised to respect the laws and customs of the Empire, not to employ foreigners and to maintain German and Latin as the official languages of government. The princes were fearful that Charles might exploit the resources of his empire to strengthen imperial authority in Germany at their expense. The 'capitulation', they hoped, would ensure that this did not happen. The princes also took the opportunity of Charles' accession to revive the constitutional experiments of the imperial reform movement. The emperor was persuaded to reform the Imperial Chamber Court. The Imperial Chamber Court was given greater independence from the Emperor, and its members were no longer to be paid by him. Again it failed to establish its credibility as a German-wide institution for the administration of justice. It soon became overburdened with work and long delays in lawsuits resulted. The Emperor was reluctant to cede any of his own legal authority to the court, whilst the princes themselves were often unwilling to permit appeals from their own courts to it. In 1521 Charles agreed to restore the Regency Council. The Emperor was to appoint its chairman and four other members. The Imperial Diet would appoint the remainder of the 22 members. Composed in this way it was clearly intended to be an instrument of the princes. The council initially developed schemes to ensure peace and order in Germany and to co-ordinate customs and monetary matters. However, it too was undermined by imperial suspicions and the lukewarm attitude of many of the princes. The latter often preferred political independence to collective action through the council. The work of the council was also hampered by the diverging interests of the princes and the cities. For his part, Charles sought to circumscribe its authority, insisting that its writ should only run when he himself was absent from Germany. Such was the impotence of the Regency Council that Charles was able to suppress it without protest in 1530. He relied on more traditional methods of governing the Empire instead of those advocated by the imperial reform movement. He worked to obtain the support of the German princes through meetings of the Imperial Diet. He encouraged the Swabian League to maintain peace and order. This it did with some success in 1522 when it defeated a revolt by the imperial knights, and in 1525 when it crushed a major peasant uprising. Clearly, then, the prospects for imperial reform came to nothing in Charles' first decade as Emperor. The princes and cities of the Empire bear some of the responsibility for this, often preferring to pursue their local self-interest to the detriment of the Imperial Chamber

Court and the Regency Council. But the Emperor played his part too. He opted to employ traditional methods of government and was suspicious of and hostile to constitutional innovation.

Charles' conservative approach to the government of the Empire was ruthlessly exposed in the later 1520s when the Lutheran movement for religious reform began to crystallise into an organised opposition to imperial authority in Germany. Several princes and numerous towns and cities of the Empire reformed their churches along the lines laid down by Martin Luther and in defiance of imperial decrees (see pages 86–8). The impact of these developments on the political situation in Germany was dramatic. The already weakened Imperial Chamber Court was further damaged by religious controversy. In 1532 Charles accepted that it was powerless to act on religious matters. More significantly, Charles' chosen instruments of government, the Imperial Diet and the Swabian League, were riven by religious division. The authority of the Diet was severely weakened by the split between Catholic and Lutheran princes and cities. By the late 1520s the Swabian League was similarly crippled by religious dissension, and it disintegrated completely in the early 1530s. To make matters worse the Lutheran princes formed an alternative league of their own (the League of Schmalkalden) in 1531. It operated as a defensive military alliance for the protection of the interests of the Lutheran princes. It even went so far as to treat with foreign powers hostile to Charles. In 1538 the Emperor's attempt to forge a countervailing league of Catholic princes came to little because it lacked the unity and resources of the old Swabian league. Furthermore, the religious Reformation in Germany gave the particularist powers of the Empire (the princes and the cities) the opportunity to reinforce their political strength and independence. The governments of reformed cities augmented their powers when they subjected the new church to municipal taxes and jurisdiction. Similarly, the princes who embraced church reform took over from the Catholic Church the administration of ecclesiastical revenues and justice. In this sense the Lutheran Reformation in Germany was not only a movement of religious renewal but also the product of the political ambitions of the German princes and cities. For this reason some historians have criticised Charles' responses to the Reformation. They argue that he failed to recognise sufficiently this vital political dimension to the spread of Lutheranism. Until the later 1540s he made no attempt to address the political and constitutional problems of imperial government. Instead he continued to negotiate with the Imperial Diet and with the German princes in the hope of finding a religious compromise which might bring the princes back to a policy of co-operation.

Charles' final attempt to reform the government of the Empire was occasioned by his military victory over the Lutheran forces in Germany at the Battle of Mühlberg in 1547. With the Lutheran princes and cities now cowed, he had one last opportunity to impose a new political settlement upon the Empire. He called a meeting of the Imperial Diet at Augsburg. It sat from September 1547 to May 1548. The Diet agreed to reform the Imperial Chamber Court, and controversial religious cases were now to be referred to the Emperor's courts. Meanwhile, many disloyal city councils were replaced by patrician governments loyal to the Emperor. However, it was the task of ensuring the loyalty of the princes that was the Emperor's greatest challenge at Augsburg. He rejected the idea of giving them representation on a revised Regency Council. Instead, recalling the Swabian League's old loyalty to the Habsburgs, he proposed the establishment of another league, albeit an extended and more powerful one. It was to have a strong central organisation and its own standing army, commanded by the Emperor. All princes and cities would be obliged to contribute towards it. Its avowed purpose was to ensure peace and order and to enforce the laws of the Empire. But, above all, it was to be responsible to the Emperor himself. Charles hoped that such an organisation would provide him with sufficient political and military strength to overcome any future challenges to his authority. However, resistance to such a league was widespread among both Lutheran and Catholic princes. They were prepared to agree to a levy on the cities to pay for an imperial army, but they were not prepared to tolerate the creation of the strong imperial monarchy in Germany which Charles' scheme implied. Therefore, the determined opposition of the princes ensured the defeat of Charles' plans. Charles lacked the resources to follow up his military victory and so he could not force such a league upon the princes. In 1552 the Emperor was driven from Germany by a rebellion of Lutheran princes, aided by French military intervention and by the neutrality of the Catholic princes. He turned away, disillusioned, from political reform and in the 1550s ceded his imperial authority to his brother Ferdinand. Ferdinand was obliged to negotiate a constitutional settlement more acceptable to the princes. This he concluded in the Treaty of Augsburg in 1555. The treaty enshrined an historic religious compromise between Lutheranism and Catholicism (see page 97). But it was also a highly political document, in which the rights and privileges of the German princes were affirmed. It was they who would decide on matters of faith and church organisation within their territories, regardless of the wishes of their subjects. The Treaty of Augsburg was a triumph for princely independence in the Empire. It also confirmed the role of the Emperor as a figurehead and not a genuine ruler. Bereft of both monarchical authority at the centre and centralised institutions of government, the Empire was condemned to a future of 'petty-statery' and destructive internal conflict. Charles undoubtedly contributed to this process of imperial decline, but it can also be argued that the Empire he inherited was already a largely ungovernable mosaic of virtually independent territories. And throughout his reign the dramatic rise of Lutheranism hugely aggravated the difficulties of administering the Empire.

4 Assessment of Charles as a Ruler

Charles faced substantial difficulties as a territorial ruler. His dominions were so extensive that it was inevitable that he was a largely absentee ruler. He was thus very dependent on the deputies and their advisers who governed on his behalf. Furthermore, each one of his realms expected him to rule in conformity with its own customs and traditions and showed little loyalty to the interests of Charles' empire as a whole. Within each of his dominions there were varying but considerable limits and checks to Charles' authority as a ruler. Each lacked political unity and uniformity. In each it was important to maintain the support and co-operation of the nobility in order to maintain effective government. How, then, did Charles respond to these circumstances? He made no serious attempt to develop empire-wide organs of government. Instead, he ruled each of his territories individually and in accordance with its own customs and practices. To this extent 'The king of all remained primarily the king of each' (J. H. Elliot). Within each part of his inheritance Charles did attempt to improve and centralise government, although in Germany his efforts came to nothing. In introducing reforms he liked to build upon existing practices and institutions. This was in many ways sensible and prudent as it provided administrative continuity and provoked less resistance from his leading subjects than more radical reform might have done. However, some historians have argued that Charles lacked the initiative and vision that would have enabled him to implement more far-reaching reforms of benefit to his individual realms and to his empire as a whole. Finally, to what extent did Charles succeed in imposing his own authority as a territorial ruler? On this issue it is difficult to generalise. Most historians contend that in Spain and the Netherlands, despite the delegation of authority to his deputies, he maintained an impressive degree of personal control. This is most evident in the areas of religion, finance and foreign policy. In Germany, on the other hand, his authority was manifestly weak. It could be concluded that his authority was greatest when he was able to rule in co-operation with the native nobility of his realms, and weakest when he was not.

Making notes on 'Charles the Ruler'

This chapter concentrates on the methods Charles employed to rule his territories and on the degree of success he enjoyed as a territorial ruler.

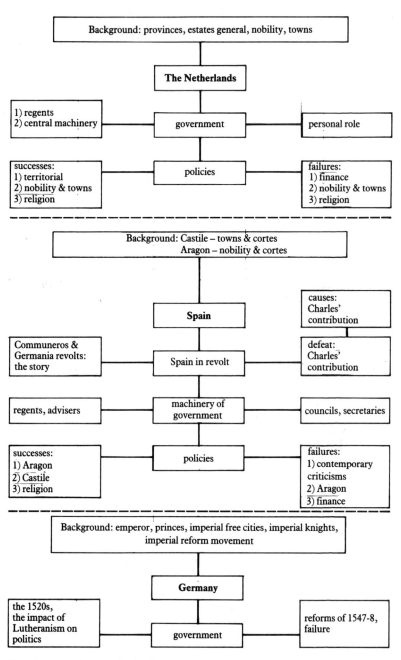

Summary – Charles the Ruler

This is a very important aspect of his career and it often receives the attention of examiners. It is therefore worthwhile taking quite detailed notes. However, it is particularly important as you read to develop your own judgements about Charles' strengths and weaknesses as a territorial ruler. Therefore, take particular note of evidence which you feel convincingly supports your own interpretation. The following headings should provide a suitable framework for your notes:

1. **The Burgundian Lands**
1.1. The Political Background
1.1.1. Identify the problems that Charles was likely to face in governing the Netherlands.
1.2. Charles' government of the Netherlands
1.2.1. Why were the Netherlands important to him?
1.2.2. What was the role of Charles' regents and how were their powers circumscribed?
1.3. Charles' Successes
1.3.1. Why do historians differ in their assessment of Charles' success in the Netherlands?
1.3.2. Assess Charles' achievement in expanding and unifying the Netherlands?
1.3.3. Why were Charles' relations with the nobility and the towns reasonably harmonious?
1.3.4. How successful was Charles in suppressing heresy?
1.4. Charles' Failures
1.4.1. Why did Charles' financial policies cause resentment?
1.4.2. What evidence is there of disloyalty to Charles in the towns and among the nobles?
1.4.3. How important do you think the failure of centralising policies was?
1.4.4. How convincing is the evidence that Charles' religious policies can be adjudged a failure?

2. **The Spanish Lands**
2.1. The Political Background
2.1.1. Identify the problems that Charles was likely to face in governing Spain.
2.2. Spain in Revolt
2.2.1. How did Charles ensure his succession and how did his subjects feel about him?
2.2.2. The effect of his imperial campaign and the appointment of Adrian of Utrecht.
2.2.3. You should be familiar with the 'story' of the *Communeros* and *Germania* revolts. But the analysis of it which follows is more important.
2.2.4. How important were the deeper economic and political causes?

2.2.6. How responsible was Charles for ending the revolts?

2.3.   The Government of Spain, 1522–56

2.3.1. How important was Spain to Charles?

2.3.2. What was the role of Charles' ministers and regents in his absence?

2.3.3. 'Conciliar' government – make notes on its origins, purposes and its *pros* and *cons*.

2.3.4. What was Cobos' role?

2.4.   Charles' Successes

2.4.1. Why is the period 1522–56 important and distinctive?

2.4.2. How did Charles achieve domestic peace in Aragon and Castile?

2.4.3. How successful was Charles in suppressing heresy?

2.5.   Charles' Weaknesses

2.5.1. What are the difficulties in assessing Charles' popularity, and how significant is the evidence of opposition to Charles' policies?

2.5.2. What criticisms can be made of Charles' financial and economic management of Spain?

3.   Germany

3.1.   The Political Background

3.1.1. How did Charles acquire Germany, what powers did the Emperor have and what were the difficulties he was likely to face in governing the Empire?

3.2.   The Imperial Reform Movement

3.2.1. What potential did the proposals of this movement have for improving the government of the Empire?

3.3.   Charles' government of Germany

3.3.1. How did Charles choose to govern Germany in the 1520s?

3.3.2. What was the impact of Lutheranism on German politics and how did Charles respond (up to the late 1540s)?

3.3.3. What did Charles propose at the Diet of Augsburg, why did this fail and what were the consequences of the failure?

4.   Assessment: What problems did Charles face as a ruler and how effectively did he respond to them?

Answering essay questions on 'Charles the Ruler'

This chapter covers Charles as a territorial ruler in the Netherlands and Spain fully, and only the political and constitutional aspects of his rule in Germany. If you are asked to give an overall assessment of Charles as Holy Roman Emperor you will need to combine the material in this chapter with coverage of his responses to the German Reformation dealt with in chapter 4.

The questions that examiners usually set on Charles as a territorial ruler can be divided into three categories.

A) The most straightforward questions demand an evaluation of Charles' rule in *one* of his territories. It is unlikely that the Netherlands will appear on its own as there is insufficient published materials available to students and they are, arguably, less important. Therefore, the most likely questions will be on Spain or Germany. The most common focus of such questions is on the degree of success or failure Charles experienced as a territorial ruler. There are three basic forms of this type of question favoured by examiners:

1. A straightforward 'why' question. These invite you to respond to a non-contentious statement. For example:

> Why was there so little internal unrest in Spain between 1522 and 1556?

Your paragraphs can be organised around a series of 'because' answers. Which 'because' factors would you use to answer this question?

2. A 'how far', 'to what extent' or 'how successful' question. For example:

> How far did Charles V solve the problems he faced as king of Spain?

Your answer should be divided into two parts. In one you should cover those areas where you feel that he was successful, and in the other those areas where you feel that he was not. Thus your paragraphs are organised around a series of 'in these respects, yes' and 'in these respects, no' answers. Which would you deal with first and why?

3. A 'challenging statement question', where a statement is made to which you are invited to agree or disagree. The statement is often, though not always, a quotation. For example:

> 'The German princes rendered Charles V powerless as Emperor.'
> Do you agree?

It is unusual to find yourself entirely and completely in agreement or disagreement with a 'challenging statement question'. To this extent, they are really 'how far', 'to what extent' questions, and can be organised accordingly. Rephrase the above question as a 'how far' question to reveal this more clearly. Of course, you might find that your answer emphasises the 'in these respects, yes' argument much more than the 'in these respects, no' argument, or *vice versa*

B) Another type of question might ask you to deal with Charles' rule in more than one of his territories. For example:

> How successful was Charles V in imposing his authority in Spain
> and in Germany?

This is quite straightforward. You should deal with each separately and towards the end draw some conclusions about Charles' success in one relative to the other. Some questions are posed in a more explicitly 'compare and contrast' format. For example:

> Discuss the view that Charles V was more successful as king of
> Spain than he was as Holy Roman Emperor.

In this case you may again deal with the two territories separately, but as you deal with the second it is important to make comparisons between Charles' success in this territory relative to his success in the first you dealt with. It is possible to structure this sort of answer more ambitiously. Different aspects of Charles' rule in both territories can be dealt with together. An obvious one is Charles' success in checking the spread of heresy. Which other themes can you think of for this answer? Bear in mind that this sort of answer requires confidence and careful planning.

C) Finally, you could be asked to write a more general assessment of Charles' career. For example:

> What were the aims of Charles V and how far did he fulfil them?

Such a question would require a substantial coverage of his role as a territorial ruler, as well as other aspects of his career. You should therefore be prepared to condense your material on Charles as a territorial ruler quite dramatically to allow for such a broad overview of his career. In such circumstances you must *select* the evidence to support your argument very carefully. Practise this before your examination.

Source-based questions on Charles the Ruler'

1 Critics of Charles' policies
Read the three short extracts on pages 26, 32 and 34.
a) What fears do the three extracts contain about the fate of Spain
   under Charles V? (*6 marks*)
b) How useful and reliable do you think the testimony of each of the

three authors is in revealing the problems Spain experienced under Charles V? (*6 marks*)

c) What do the three extracts reveal about the relationship between Charles and his representatives in Spain? (*6 marks*)

d) The extracts on pages 32 and 34 concern Spanish finances. To what extent do you think that they accurately portray Spain's economic and financial position under Charles V? Refer to the evidence presented in this chapter (*7 marks*)

2 Charles' views on government

Read the two extracts on pages 27 and 28.

a) What evidence is there in the extract on page 27 of Charles' desire to maintain personal control over the government of Spain? (*2 marks*)

b) Referring to the extract on page 28, explain in your own words why Charles 'included the heads of both parties' in Philip's ministry. (*2 marks*)

c) What do the extracts reveal about Charles' attitude towards the Duke of Alva? (*4 marks*)

d) Why do you think that the second extract was sent confidentially, whereas the first was not? (*2 marks*)

CHAPTER 3

Charles the Dynast

1 The Family

The empire of Charles V has been portrayed by some historians, notably by one of his leading biographers, Karl Brandi, as the triumph of the dynastic idea in politics. They mean by this that the Habsburg family was at the heart of Charles' imperial reign and ambitions. The dynastic ideal is apparent in his reign in several inter-related ways. Firstly, he took great pride in his Habsburg lineage. Therefore his actions can often be best understood as an effort to preserve his inheritance and, with it, the achievements of his ancestors. Secondly, Charles' empire was dynastic because it was based on family inheritance and not, like many other historical empires, on conquest. (The Americas are something of an exception here.) The Netherlands, Spain and the Austrian dukedoms all fell to him through legal inheritance. As we have seen (page 34), even the Holy Roman Empire was very much a Habsburg patrimony. Thirdly, the Habsburg family formed the foundation of Charles' system of government. He did not attempt to weld his disparate territories together under centralised control. Instead, he employed members of his family to govern his individual dominions on his behalf. The historian H. G. Koenigsberger has described his system of administering his empire in the following terms:

> He governed it like the head of the great sixteenth century merchant houses, where the junior members of the family served as heads of the foreign branches of the firm.

Lastly, in foreign policy, Charles sought to exploit marriage alliances between the Habsburgs and other leading families in Europe in order to extend the influence of his dynasty and to establish international relations favourable to his interests. In the words of Karl Brandi:

> Thus all Europe might be conveniently drawn into a great web, bound together by brothers, sisters, children, nephews, nieces of the Emperor.

Therefore, the dynastic idea was of central importance to Charles' whole political outlook. It has been contended that his primary aim was, in short, the greatness of the House of Habsburg.

a) Ferdinand

The most pressing family question that Charles faced when he suc-

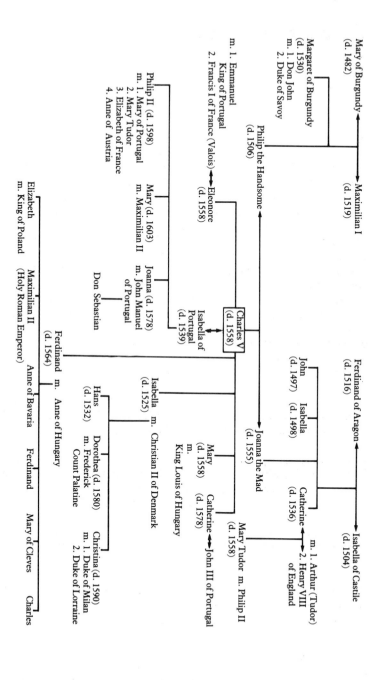

The Dynasty of Charles V

ceeded to the Spanish thrones in 1516 was how to deal with his 14-year-old brother, Ferdinand. As we have seen (page 25), many of his Castilian subjects regarded Ferdinand as a preferable heir in Spain. Charles decided to have his brother removed from Spain, but in the longer term it was essential that he be given an inheritance of his own. He was widely regarded as an important prince in his own right, and Charles was anxious to avoid having a disinherited malcontent at the heart of the Habsburg family. Negotiations on a settlement for Ferdinand dragged on until 1522. Ferdinand was eager to bid for the imperial title in 1519. However, Charles coveted the title for himself and blocked his brother's nomination. Charles was also determined to retain control over his Spanish and Burgundian inheritance. This left the Habsburg Austrian dukedoms in central Europe. In the Treaty of Brussels of 1522 Charles renounced his claims to them and Ferdinand was made the Archduke of Austria, with full hereditary rights. Ferdinand, in turn, renounced any claim to Spain and the Netherlands. His position in central Europe had already been strengthened when the prospects of attaining the Habsburg lands had enabled him to secure the hand of the daughter of the king of Hungary and Bohemia in marriage in 1521. By 1527 he had succeeded to both kingdoms. By the Treaty of Brussels it was also agreed that Ferdinand would deputise for Charles as Holy Roman Emperor. He would gain considerable prestige from such a role. Furthermore, Charles agreed to work to secure the succession to the Holy Roman Empire for his brother. This he promised to do once he had been formally crowned as Emperor by the Pope. This did not take place until 1530. Charles then moved to fulfil his promise. In order to do so it was necessary to persuade the German electors to elect Ferdinand to the title of King of the Romans, a title given to the agreed successor of an incumbent Emperor. Traditionally, this title was given to the Emperor's son, but after much bribery and persuasion Charles arranged for the coronation of his brother in January 1531. It is not entirely clear from the available evidence how Ferdinand viewed this dynastic settlement arrived at in the 1520s. However, he had reason to be relatively contented. The lands of Austria, Bohemia and Hungary made him a substantial territorial prince. In fact, they formed the basis of the Austrian Habsburg monarchy until 1918. He anticipated succeeding Charles as Holy Roman Emperor and then securing the subsequent succession to the imperial throne for his own family. When Charles later attempted to thwart Ferdinand's imperial ambitions for his family a serious rift developed between the two brothers (see pages 59–63).

b) Spain and the Netherlands

The role of the Habsburg family in Spain was more straightforward. When Ferdinand of Aragon died in 1516, the legitimate successor to

Castile and Aragon was Charles' mother, Joanna. However, she was mentally unstable. It is probably the case that she was, indeed, unfit to govern, although such a claim undoubtedly suited Charles and his Burgundian advisers. In 1517 Charles obtained from her the right to govern Spain; although at first he used her name as well as his own in official documents, she was excluded from political and dynastic affairs. In a letter to her guardian in 1520 Charles commented:

> It seems to me that the best and most suitable thing for you to do is to make sure that no person speaks with her Majesty, for no good could come of it.

It was inevitable that Charles would be absent from Spain for considerable periods of time. This made the choice of a wife who would be able to deputise for him particularly important. His engagement to the five-year-old Mary Tudor in 1522 was distinctly unpromising in this respect (see page 56). Earlier Charles had been tempted by the prospect of a marriage alliance with the Valois dynasty of France. The foreign policy advantages of a compact with one of Europe's most powerful ruling houses were attractive, and a dynastic alignment with France might enable him to end decades of war with France and secure peace in Christendom. However, in 1526 Charles married his 23-year-old first cousin, Princess Isabella of Portugal. The benefits of the marriage were obvious. Charles would receive a very substantial dowry from the wealthy Avis dynasty of Portugal. And he appreciated that his Spanish subjects were much better disposed to a Portuguese alliance than a French one. They felt a greater feeling of kinship with the neighbouring Portuguese. A Portuguese alliance was also in keeping with the dynastic policies of Charles' widely revered grandparents, Ferdinand and Isabella. Charles' wife served him loyally and effectively as regent in Spain. This he acknowledged in a letter of 1536:

> 1 Her Most Serene Highness, the very noble and most able Empress and Queen doña Isabel, Our most dear and very well-beloved wife, possesses excellent virtues, prudence and great qualities. The love which she has for these kingdoms and their
> 5 subjects is the same as We have; and she is as a consequence beloved by them, revered and obeyed. We have experience of her good and praiseworthy government and administration in our absences from these kingdoms.

It was, therefore, a great personal and political loss when Isabella died in 1539. However, the marriage had produced three children; Philip (born in 1527), Mary (1528) and Joanna (1535). It was, of course, the birth of a male heir which most pleased Charles and his subjects. His official announcement of Philip's birth in 1527 captures both the pride of the father and of the monarch:

1 As I am aware of the happiness and joy that it will bring you all, I
   hereby announce that it has pleased our Lord to give a son to our
   Empress and Queen, my very dear and most beloved wife. The
   happy event has taken place today, Tuesday the 21st of May. I
5 trust in God that he will serve Him and my kingdoms.

Charles named his child Philip in remembrance of his father, apparently against the wishes of his Spanish subjects, who would have preferred
to remember Ferdinand of Aragon. Despite his many absences, Charles
took a great interest in the young prince's development and ensured
that he was well tutored in the arts of government. Philip was declared
regent, in name at least, immediately upon the death of his mother in
1539. When he reached the age of 16 in 1543 he was given full rights as
regent in Spain, including the command of his ministers. For the
remainder of Charles' life he governed Spain in the Emperor's absence.
Charles urged Philip to maintain good relations with his uncle,
Ferdinand, and with Ferdinand's son, Maximilian. He proposed, also,
that Philip should defer to the more experienced Ferdinand in the
foreign affairs of the Habsburgs. Finally, Charles decided to maintain
the Habsburgs' dynastic alliance with Portugal. He arranged for the
marriage of Philip to the latter's cousin, Mary of Portugal, in 1543.
However, she died in 1545, after giving birth to a son, Don Carlos.
   When Charles was declared of age in the Netherlands in 1515 the
choice of a blood-relative to govern there in his absence was obvious.
His aunt, Margaret of Austria, widow of the Duke of Savoy, had
headed the government of the Netherlands almost continuously since
the death of Charles' father. She had supervised his upbringing in the
Netherlands and had encouraged him to claim the Spanish throne at the
expense of his brother Ferdinand. From 1515 to her death in 1530 she
ruled the Netherlands as Governess-General. Her presence ensured
continuity in the administration, whilst she also proved to be a valuable
source of counsel to Charles on wider imperial matters. Charles was
fortunate that when she died his sister Mary, the widowed and
impecunious Queen of Hungary, was available to replace her. Mary had
lost the greater part of Hungary to Turkish occupation and now lacked
a suitable role in the Habsburg dynastic system. She was also unencum-
bered by a husband who might demand loyalty other than to the
Habsburgs. Mary, too, became one of Charles' most trusted advisers on
foreign and imperial affairs. She also acted as an arbiter in disagree-
ments that arose within the Habsburg family. Charles had long been
determined that the Netherlands should be passed on to Philip. He
regarded them with intense family pride and naturally wished to see
them secured for his only son. In 1550 Philip was formally recognised
in the Netherlands as Charles' successor. When Charles abdicated in
1555 Mary stepped down as Governess-General and Philip's reign as
Duke of Burgundy commenced.

c) Portugal

The importance of the family in the reign of Charles V is evident not only in the government of his own dominions but also in his relations with other powers. Marriage was for Charles an important instrument of foreign policy. Habsburg relations with the Portuguese House of Avis were periodically cemented by marriage ties. Apart from Charles and Philip's Portuguese marriages, other Habsburgs played their part also. In 1517 Charles put an end to a love affair between his eldest sister, Eleonore, and a German prince. Instead, he arranged her betrothal to her elderly uncle, Emmanuel, King of Portugal. In 1521 she both gave birth to a daughter and was widowed. The new king, John III, Eleonore's stepson, was married in 1525 to Charles' youngest sister, Katherine. John lived until 1557. In the meantime, in 1542 ties with Portugal were further strengthened, and indeed complicated, by the marriage of Charles' seven-year-old daughter, Joanna, to the heir to the Portuguese throne, John Manuel. John Manuel never succeeded to the throne but he left the next Portuguese heir when Joanna gave birth to Don Sebastian in the year of her husband's death (1554). In these ways the royal houses of Spain and Portugal were bound closely together. To this extent, it can be argued that Charles laid the foundations for the union of the crowns of Spain and Portugal in 1581. However, he also created a situation of some dynastic complexity that was to rebound on him in his retirement. When King John died in 1557 both Katherine and Joanna laid claim to the Portuguese regency. Charles backed Katherine as regent, as he had duties for Joanna to perform in Spain, but at the cost of some ill-feeling within the family.

d) France

Charles saw France as another target for dynastic advances. France was the major power in Europe outside his empire and throughout his reign their relationship was punctuated by war (see section 2). Therefore dynastic ties with France might curtail conflict between the Habsburgs and the French, and so bring peace to Christendom. It might also check French support for Charles' Protestant and Muslim opponents. The most obvious means of bringing the two countries together was by Charles marrying into the French Valois dynasty. This he agreed to in the 1516 Treaty of Noyon, when he promised to marry the King of France's daughter, who at the time was less than one-year-old. However, when Charles defeated the French king, Francis I, in the election for the imperial title in 1519, Franco-Habsburg relations became strained. The Anglo-Habsburg alliance of 1520 put further obstacles in the way of a Franco-Habsburg marriage accord. In the first half of the 1520s a state of war existed between Charles and the French. The Treaty of Madrid in 1526 brought a brief suspension of hostilities and marriage negotiations were resumed. However, by this time Charles had committed himself to a Portuguese marriage, and it was therefore agreed that Charles' sister, Eleonore, should marry the French king. The marriage did not take place until 1530, following a second peace with France in 1529. Charles hoped that a Habsburg Queen of France would help the Habsburgs and the Valois to overcome their mutual suspicions and conflicts. However, war persisted intermittently for the rest of Charles' reign. Eleonore was largely ignored by her womanising husband and she secured no significant influence over the formulation of French foreign policy (she died in 1558). However, Charles continued to hope that a further Habsburg-Valois marriage might improve relations. In the 1530s and 40s he initiated prolonged, if ultimately abortive, negotiations for a further marriage alliance. The bargaining counters were in this case the children of Charles and Ferdinand and those of Francis I. In 1540, for example, Charles proposed that his daughter Mary marry the French king's younger son, Charles Duke of Orléans. However, these discussions reached their most remarkable climax in the Habsburg-Valois Peace of Crépy, in 1544. Charles offered to give the Duke of Orléans either Milan or the Netherlands as a dowry on his marriage to a Habsburg princess. If Charles nominated Anne, Ferdinand's daughter, the duke would receive Milan; if he nominated his own daughter, Mary, the dowry would be the Low Countries. Both Milan and the Netherlands were highly prized by Charles, and they each constituted a vital part of his existing empire. That he could contemplate sacrificing either in pursuing a marriage alliance with the French testifies to the importance he attached to such a dynastic arrangement. However, Charles' scheme collapsed when the Duke of Orléans died in September 1545. The Emperor was therefore saved from making the difficult decision as to which of his possessions to abandon to the French. His last years were plagued by French diplomatic and military hostility. Therefore, it can be argued, in the case of France at least, that Charles overestimated the value of dynastic diplomacy. He was unrealistic on two counts. Firstly, he believed too readily in the sincerity of French marriage negotiations. The French invariably hesitated to commit themselves. Instead, they kept negotiations open in order to keep alive their claims to sovereignty over territories they disputed with the Habsburgs (the duchy of Milan, in particular). Secondly, Charles showed some naïvety in hoping that marriage alliances on their own might significantly help to overcome fundamental differences which divided the Habsburgs and the Valois. In reality, of course, they did not necessarily have any effect. The fact that France had a Habsburg queen from 1530 to the death of Francis in 1547 was no assurance of peace and harmony between the rival royal houses.

e) Denmark

Charles encountered rather different dynastic difficulties in the northern kingdoms of Denmark, Norway and Sweden. His problems here were not really of his own making. In 1515 his second sister, Isabella, married Christian II, the King of Denmark (which included the kingdom of Norway). The royal couple had four children. Christian was an unscrupulous adventurer who treated his wife with disloyalty and cruelty. He was also intensely ambitious and wished to extend his rule to the kingdom of Sweden. In 1520 his armies defeated the Swedes. He seized the throne and crushed internal opposition with brutality. The Swedes, led by Gustav Vasa, rebelled, and in 1523 drove Christian out of the country. Christian had solicited support from his Habsburg relations in his efforts to retain Sweden. Charles was tempted to support him and so extend the influence of his dynasty in the north. However, the economy of the Netherlands was very much dependent on trade with the northern kingdoms. Therefore Margaret, the Governess-General of the Netherlands, persuaded Charles to avoid jeopardising trade with the Swedes by furnishing aid to his brother-in-law.

Christian became equally unpopular in Denmark and in 1523 his own subjects rose against him. He was driven out of the kingdom and replaced by his uncle, Frederick of Holstein. Christian and his family were now exiles and came under the care of their Habsburg relations. Isabella died in 1526. From the beginning Charles vetoed any idea of helping to restore Christian to the Danish throne. Trade between the Netherlands and Denmark was important and, again, Margaret emphasised to Charles the damage that would be done to the trade of the Netherlands by Habsburg support for Christian. The Habsburgs even discussed with King Frederick the possibility of a marriage alliance between his son and one of Isabella and Christian's daughters. Such an alliance would have returned the Danish ruling family to the Habsburg dynastic orbit, but Charles decided against allying with a king who had usurped his own blood-relations in the first place. In 1530 Christian met with Charles to plead for Habsburg support in an attempt to regain Denmark by force. He pledged to renounce his earlier Protestantism and to rule Denmark as the emperor's vassal. Charles again refused, and in 1531 Christian's invasion of Denmark ended in disaster. He was taken prisoner and remained imprisoned in Copenhagen until his death in 1559. In theory Charles continued to uphold the claims of Christian's children to their Danish inheritance, but the dynastic claims of the Habsburgs in the north were low in his list of priorities and in practice he did nothing to further their claims. When King Frederick died in 1533 and was succeeded by his son, Christian III, Charles continued to acquiesce in the usurpation of his family's rights in Denmark. In addition, he turned a blind eye to Mary of Hungary's encouragement of close relations between the Netherlands and Denmark. His failure to promote actively the dynastic interests of the Habsburgs in the northern kingdoms was, as H. G. Koenigsberger points out, 'a victory of the political and economic over the dynastic concept of empire' but 'the emperor accepted it only with great reluctance'. The reasons why he accepted his family's dispossession in the north are clear. He was pressed by his advisers in the Netherlands to safeguard their trade in the north, Christian III was too notoriously unreliable to use as an instrument of family policy, and Charles had more pressing problems elsewhere.

f) England

England loomed larger than the northern kingdoms in Charles' dynastic ambitions. It was a more significant European power, well used to an important role in international affairs. There were already very close economic ties between England and the Habsburg Netherlands; the Flemish cloth industry depended on English wool exports. Moreover, there was a history of close Anglo-Spanish relations. Both countries shared a suspicion of France. And in the reign of Henry VII (1485–1509) Anglo-Spanish relations had been cemented by the marriage of Charles' aunt, Catherine of Aragon, the daughter of Ferdinand of Aragon and Isabella of Castile, to Henry VII's sons; first to Arthur in 1501 and then to the future Henry VIII in 1509. Catherine gave birth to a daughter, Mary Tudor, in 1516. The princess's claim to the English throne should her father die without a male heir ensured the continuing dynastic interest of the Habsburgs in England. In Charles' early years the Anglo-Habsburg alignment of diplomatic and family interests was maintained, and in 1522 the Emperor was engaged to his cousin, Mary Tudor, as part of an Anglo-Habsburg alliance against France. However, the marriage was somewhat improbable, as the English princess was only five-years-old. Henry VIII was highly offended when Charles married a Portuguese princess in 1526. Nevertheless, recent history suggested that Charles could anticipate a future of close relations between the House of Habsburg and the House of Tudor.

In 1527 the relationship between the Habsburgs and England was rudely shattered when Henry VIII decided that he wished to divorce Catherine of Aragon on the grounds that the marriage was invalid as Catherine was his brother's widow. He was not able to obtain the divorce until 1533. English historians have taken a great interest in unravelling Henry's real motives in pursuing the divorce. Here we may mention two major reasons. Firstly, he had lost interest in Catherine and had fallen in love with Anne Boleyn. Secondly, he was convinced that Catherine would never provide him with a male heir who could ensure the future of the Tudor dynasty in England. His determination to divorce Catherine appalled Charles V for a variety of reasons. In the years leading up to her divorce Catherine was maltreated and humiliated by her husband. This affronted his strong feelings of obligation towards members of his family. Catherine's daughter Mary was similarly ill-used and the grounds of Henry's projected divorce threatened the legitimacy of her birth and her claim to the succession. Her claim to the throne was, in fact, formally annulled a year after the divorce in the Act of Succession. Moreover, Charles feared that the divorce might detach England from its traditional leanings to Spain and align it more with his enemy, France. Finally, it became apparent to Henry that the only way he could obtain a divorce was by rejecting the authority of the Pope, as by church law his divorce required papal approval. When this was not forthcoming he went ahead with the divorce without papal sanction in 1533. He then proceeded to reform the Church in England, abolishing papal supremacy and establishing the king as head of the Church of England. From Charles' point of view Henry was taking the English Church in a heretically Protestant direction. This he condemned out of Catholic conviction, and it strengthened his determination to protect his Catholic cousin, Mary Tudor, and her prospects for the succession after Henry's death. He was particularly fearful of Protestantism triumphing in England as he felt it could easily infect his subjects across the Channel in the Netherlands.

The issue of Henry's divorce undoubtedly did much to damage Anglo-Habsburg relations, at least until the death of Catherine of Aragon in 1536. Henry sent his ambassadors to persuade Charles to accept the divorce, but the Emperor was unrelenting in his opposition. Henry issued learned justifications for his action, invoking legal and scriptural authority. Charles, in response, instructed the scholars and theologians of Spain to refute the King of England's case. However, before Henry was driven to a breach with Rome, Charles found that his most effective means of frustrating Henry's designs lay in exerting pressure on the Pope. His military successes against the French in Italy in the second half of the 1520s (see page 70) and his triumph over papal independence following the 'Sack of Rome' (see page 70) ensured that Pope Clement VII (1523–34) effectively became a pawn of the Habsburgs. In 1529 he signed the Treaty of Barcelona with the Emperor, pledging to remain loyal to Habsburg policy. Henry VIII's prospects of obtaining papal approval for his divorce were now scotched. He married a pregnant Anne Boleyn in January 1533, was divorced without papal assent in May, and in September Anne gave birth to the future Elizabeth I. The birth was a further cause of foreboding to Charles, as it further jeopardised Mary's prospects for the succession. However, by 1537 Mary's position had become even more precarious. In 1536 Henry had Anne Boleyn executed for treasonable adultery. He immediately married his third wife, Jane Seymour, who gave birth to a male heir, the future Edward VI, in October 1537. Edward and his descendants now appeared to be the sole legitimate heirs in England.

There was, then, ample cause for conflict between the Habsburgs and Tudors over the treatment of Queen Catherine and Princess Mary. However, even before the death of Catherine in 1536, it became evident that the dynastic imperatives of Charles V had to be reconciled with wider political and economic considerations. In 1528 he rejected a proposal for military action against England as a means of protecting his family interests there. Margaret, the Governess-General of the Netherlands, helped to dissuade him as she feared the damage a loss of Anglo-Burgundian trade would do to the economy of the Netherlands. Economic considerations continued to influence the emperor. For example, in 1533 he discouraged Pope Clement VII from implementing a papal interdict against England, pointing out that it would 'disturb her intercourse (trade) with Spain and the Netherlands'. Other factors reinforced economic ones and dissuaded Charles from taking retaliatory action against Henry VIII. In the first half of the 1530s he was distracted by the Protestant and Muslim threats to his dominions. He realised that the more aggressive he was towards England the more likely he was to drive Henry VIII into the French camp, and therefore he issued instructions to his ambassadors to be conciliatory towards the English. In 1535 he unsuccessfully suggested to Henry that some sort of compromise over the divorce issue might be found at a meeting of a General Council of the Church.

The prospects for Anglo-Habsburg relations were greatly improved when Catherine of Aragon died in January 1536. Habsburg grievances against Henry VIII for his shabby treatment of Catherine were now more easily shelved. Charles was, of course, still eager to uphold the inheritance rights of Princess Mary. But he also wished to return Habsburg-Tudor relations to a firmer dynastic footing, particularly as war with France now appeared inevitable. In February 1536 he proposed a renewal of Anglo-Habsburg friendship and that he and Henry should jointly endeavour to find a husband for Mary Tudor. His overtures were rebuffed as Henry wished to secure a position of neutrality in the coming Habsburg-Valois war. In 1538 he tried to win Henry VIII over to another dynastic scheme and he proposed that Henry marry his adolescent cousin, Christina, widow of the Duke of Milan and daughter of the imprisoned Christian II of Denmark. Commentators have noted a somewhat heartless and cynical element to this plan. Having humiliated his first wife and executed his second Henry was not exactly the ideal partner for a young Habsburg princess. Fortunately, perhaps, for Christina, the English king again refused Charles' dynastic offer. However, Anglo-Habsburg relations remained reasonably harmonious. In 1543 a brief alliance was forged, in which Anglo-Burgundian trade agreements were prominent, and in 1544 Charles was given reason to become more optimistic about the dynastic prospects of the Habsburgs in England. Henry VIII passed a new Succession Act in that year, in which he legitimated Mary and

Elizabeth and granted them the succession after Edward and his heirs. The line of Edward, Mary then Elizabeth was confirmed by Henry's will when he died in 1547. When the boy-king Edward succeeded to the throne, Charles aimed to remain on good terms with his government and to protect Mary Tudor's rights in England. When the English government began to introduce radical Protestant changes to the English Church, Charles was given considerable cause for concern. Plans were laid to remove Mary from England in an emergency. However, Edward's ministers had no wish to alienate the Habsburgs, and Mary's position in England remained relatively secure until just before the death of Edward in 1553. The dying king was persuaded to disinherit his two half-sisters and pass the crown to Lady Jane Grey, the daughter-in-law of a leading noble. When Edward died in July she was proclaimed queen. In the event, Jane Grey was swept from power in nine days by forces loyal to Mary. Mary was immediately crowned amidst considerable enthusiasm in the country. Thus Charles V saw one of his longest-standing dynastic ambitions realised. His cousin was now Queen of England. Her accession opened up tremendous opportunities for the ageing Emperor (see pages 62–4).

g) The Succession to Charles

Undoubtedly, the greatest dynastic crisis that Charles V faced in his reign occurred at the heart of the Habsburg family. We have already seen how the Treaty of Brussels in 1522, and the crowning of Ferdinand as King of the Romans in 1531, appeared to Ferdinand to guarantee the succession to the imperial title to his own descendants. However in the later 1540s Charles began to suggest within his family circle that the succession to the Empire after Ferdinand's death might well revert to his own branch of the family. This meant that his son Philip, and not Ferdinand's son Maximilian, could become King of the Romans under Ferdinand, and so succeed to the imperial dignity on Ferdinand's death. This scenario was referred to as the 'Spanish Succession'. Charles cherished the idea of perpetuating his empire undivided under his own heirs, even if the Holy Roman Empire was temporarily detached during Ferdinand's reign. The revelation of Charles' new plans occasioned a family quarrel which lasted from late 1547 to 1551 and which clouded family relationships for the rest of Charles' life. Rumours of the quarrel spread quickly round the courts of Europe, receiving some embellishment as they went. It was suggested by some, for example, that Charles really intended to make Philip, and not Ferdinand, his immediate successor as Emperor. Such stories of Habsburg division were welcomed and eagerly recycled by Charles' opponents in Europe, notably the French and the German Protestants.

Allegory on the abdication of Charles V by F. Francken II

In the summer of 1550 a family conference was called at Augsburg to try to resolve family differences over the imperial succession. A memorandum, in the form of questions and answers, drafted as a working paper for this conference provides some insight into the issues at stake:

1   Q   'It is necessary to determine the [further] succession during the lifetime of Charles and Ferdinand?'

      A   'Yes; in order to avoid the election of a weakling or a heretic.'

      Q   'What is required, in a successor?'

5   A   'Besides knightly qualities, first and foremost great wealth, since the Empire possesses none of its own, but has greedy neighbours such as the French and the Turk.'

      Q   'Where is a suitable candidate to be found?'

      A   'Only in the House of Austria, as a glance over a list of the

10   German princes at once reveals.'

      Q   'Is it necessary to secure the imperial dignity to this House?'

      A   'Yes; for its members have always been ready to pour out their treasure for Christendom. And the principle forbidding hereditary succession would not be violated thereby, because there

15   would still be an election, and the best candidate would be chosen.'

      Q   'Who is better fitted to be Emperor, at present, Maximilian or Philip?'

      A   'The essential point is that these two princes should remain in

20   the closest association. Maximilian knows the German princes and their language, and has had valuable experience in peace and war. Philip's realms are far-flung; he is unfamiliar with German and the Germans, and may even be unpopular among them because of the Spanish soldiery. But Italy, the other arm of the

25   Empire and the seat of the Imperial dignity and the papacy, can be defended only from Germany, just as France can be held within bounds only from Germany and the Low Countries. As regards Philip's Spanish speech and upbringing, the same was once true of Ferdinand, who nonetheless became a good Ger-

30   man. Under the guidance of his father, Philip would give a free hand to all his states. The plan [to make him Emperor] presents difficulties, of course; but had not Ferdinand's election as King of the Romans? The decisive factor would always be a complete understanding between Charles and Ferdinand, and their sons.'

However, there was little evidence of the spirit of understanding, called for in the memorandum, when the main protagonists arrived in Augsburg to put their cases in person. Charles and Philip outlined the advantages of the 'Spanish succession'. Ferdinand was stubborn and suspicious. He invoked previous agreements and the feelings of the

German electors to justify Maximilian's succession. Maximilian acted haughtily and avoided his cousin, Philip, altogether. Charles' sister, Mary of Hungary, acted energetically as a go-between and edged the two parties towards an agreement. She backed the 'Spanish succession' and pointed out to Ferdinand that Charles had sacrificed his own son in Ferdinand's favour when he had arranged Ferdinand's election as King of the Romans in 1531. However, as an inducement to Ferdinand she suggested that, in the longer term, Philip should be succeeded in turn by Maximilian (the 'alternating succession'). Ferdinand was persuaded to go along with the compromise, and in March 1551 he formally accepted the 'alternating succession' in the Augsburg Agreement. In addition, to guarantee that his son could eventually expect to succeed Philip, he was given further promises. Philip pledged that he would not interfere in Ferdinand's imperial business. Charles undertook to provide resources in future conflicts between Ferdinand and the Ottoman Sultan. Finally, it was agreed that Philip should marry one of Ferdinand's daughters. However, it soon became apparent that the parties to the Augsburg Agreement had not committed themselves entirely in good faith. Maximilian, indeed, had only given his verbal consent, refusing to enter into a written agreement. He continued to conspire with the German electors in order to smooth his own path to the imperial throne. Ferdinand blocked attempts by Charles to arrange for the formal acknowledgement of Philip's rights in Germany. In 1552, when Charles was faced with a major revolt in the Empire, Ferdinand did little to help him. Soon Charles and Philip acted, too, as if the agreement was a dead letter. They ignored the provisions which stipulated Philip's marriage into Ferdinand's family. Instead, after exploring the possibility of a Portuguese marriage, in 1554 Philip married the new English queen, Mary Tudor. In backing the English marriage alliance, Charles recognised that the unity of the Habsburg empire was now likely to be irrevocably broken. Ferdinand's dynasty would be founded on a central European power-base and the imperial title. Philip and his heirs would inherit a western European empire, comprising Spain (including Italy and the Americas), the Netherlands and England. Therefore, in 1555 Philip formally renounced his right to succeed Ferdinand to the imperial title. In return, the duchy of Milan was transferred from imperial to Spanish jurisdiction. However, the English dynastic initiative failed when Mary died without heir in 1558.

What, then, lay behind this deterioration in Charles' relations with Ferdinand and his family? Charles clearly underestimated Ferdinand's ambitions for his own family. This misjudgement may have owed something to the fact that, throughout his life, he had only intermittent personal contact with his brother. Moreover, there were quite compelling political and strategic considerations which motivated him to press Philip's claim to the imperial succession. Charles appreciated that the position of the Habsburgs in Germany would be greatly strengthened if the Emperor also ruled Spain and the Netherlands; military and economic support from Spain and the Netherlands would help the Emperor to confront the ambitions of the princes inside Germany and the threat from the Ottoman Empire from without. Lastly, Charles invested his family pride very much in his son Philip, for whom he wished as great a future as possible. This was obviously best achieved by maintaining an undivided dynastic structure with Philip at its head.

Charles' plans were, then, understandable and not without merit. However, what they lacked was an appreciation of the formidable obstacles which lay in their path. Firstly, Ferdinand believed that the imperial succession had already been secured for his own line and interpreted Charles' scheme as a breach of promise. His son, Maximilian, was an ambitious young prince who had little affection for Charles or Philip and was determined that he should succeed his father. The dynastic ambitions of Ferdinand and Maximilian were greatly strengthened by the knowledge that they had the support of political opinion in Germany. Maximilian was brought up as a German prince and was seen as being far preferable as a successor to Ferdinand than Philip, a foreign Spanish prince. The German princes were also sensitive to Charles attempting to dictate the line of imperial succession, regardless of their own electoral rights. In addition, religious issues further undermined Charles' plans. In the late 1540s and the early 1550s a revolt gathered momentum in Germany in opposition to Charles' efforts to impose orthodox Catholicism throughout the Empire. Ferdinand, and Maximilian in particular, were known to be more sympathetic to the feelings of the Protestant opposition in Germany. The idea of Philip, perceived as a typically fanatical Spanish Catholic, inheriting the imperial title appalled both Protestant and moderate Catholic opinion in Germany. Lastly, the French were prepared actively to support Ferdinand's succession plans for several reasons; to embarrass their great rival Charles, to weaken and divide the House of Habsburg and to assist their Protestant allies in Germany in their opposition to Philip's succession.

h) Assessment

To what extent, then, did Charles rule according to dynastic principles, and how successful was he when he chose to apply them? The importance of the family is most evident in his system of government. Here he enjoyed considerable success. Members of his family were securely established as his deputies in his individual dominions. For the most part, they served the Emperor and the House of Habsburg with fidelity. The notable exception was Ferdinand and Maximilian's disloyalty in the 1550s. The use of the family in the pursuit of Habsburg foreign policy was beset with greater difficulties. There were invariably a variety of factors, besides dynastic ones, which affected Charles' relations with other countries. For example, in the case of the northern kingdoms and England we have seen how important economic considerations were, and how they forced Charles to curb his dynastic ambitions. Indeed, it can be argued that Charles' dynastic foreign policy was only successful when it reinforced existing affinities and alliances, as with Portugal. On the other hand, dynastic relations with France were constantly bedevilled by deep-seated rivalries and enmities. However, Charles' greatest dynastic regret was undoubtedly his failure to bequeath an undivided empire to his son. He fervently believed that passing on his empire intact to Philip was the best way of ensuring the future greatness of the House of Habsburg. But historians have tended to be less harsh on the Emperor for this than he was on himself. They argue that the division of the empire between his son and his brother made much sense. In many ways his own empire was too unwieldy in its size and diversity. Philip's succession to Spain and the Netherlands appeared to provide him with a more compact and manageable inheritance. Furthermore, Philip's marriage to Mary Tudor in 1554 was potentially a masterstroke by the Emperor. Philip, it has been contended, would rule an empire of three logical units; England and the Netherlands, Spain and Italy, and America. This scheme was only undone by the death of Mary without issue in 1558. Such, inevitably, were the pitfalls of dynastic politics.

2 The Habsburg–Valois Rivalry

a) Introduction

Charles spent much of his reign at war with the Valois dynasty of France. To some extent he was continuing an existing conflict; Spain and the empire had been periodically at war with France over their rival dynastic claims in Italy since 1494. Charles' inheritance made a continuation of conflict likely. The reason for this was partly personal. Charles was a proud young monarch, who felt that his mighty empire conferred upon him political leadership in Christian Europe. His rival, Francis I, succeeded to the French throne in 1515, at the age of 21. From the beginning, he was anxious to make a name for himself and to pursue fame by continuing the expansionist foreign policy of his predecessors. He was resentful of his young Habsburg rival and determined to resist Charles' claims to supremacy in Europe. This personal jealousy was greatly intensified in 1519 when Francis was defeated by Charles in the contest to become Holy Roman Emperor. Conflict was also likely for strategic reasons. When Charles acquired the Empire in 1519 France found itself effectively encircled by Habsburg territories; by Spain in the south and by the Netherlands and Germany in the north and east. French feelings of vulnerability were further intensified by the Anglo-Habsburg alliances of 1520 and 1522. Therefore, the French aimed to break out of Habsburg encirclement by challenging the dynasty's claims in Italy, and their control of Milan in particular.

However, such strategic considerations do not provide a sufficient explanation of the Habsburg–Valois wars during the reign of Charles V. After all, the wars commenced decades earlier, before the encirclement of France in 1519. Arguably, the wars were, above all, dynastic. They derived from the rival dynastic claims of the House of Habsburg and the House of Valois. The wars were fought over disputed territories, but the combatants were more interested in their family rights and in the prospects of dynastic aggrandizement than in territorial expansion for its own sake. It was this dynastic rivalry that led the historian G. R. Elton to compare the bitterness of the Habsburg–Valois conflict to 'the virulence of family quarrels'. The House of Valois contested the Duke of Burgundy's control over Flanders and Artois, whilst the Burgundian dukes claimed Tournai, which was held by France (see map, page 15). Furthermore, the Burgundian dukes had lost their historic family lands to France in 1477. Their recovery was an emotive issue for them. In his early years as duke of Burgundy, Charles was very much preoccupied with restoring his ancestral lands. Italy provided the most dangerous point of dynastic conflict. As King of Aragon, Charles inherited Naples

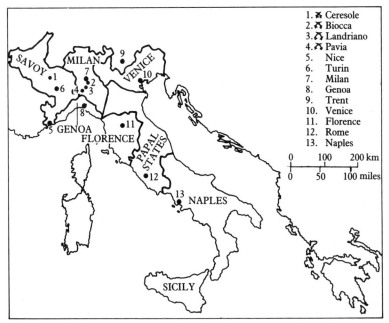

1. ⚔ Ceresole
2. ⚔ Biocca
3. ⚔ Landriano
4. ⚔ Pavia
5. Nice
6. Turin
7. Milan
8. Genoa
9. Trent
10. Venice
11. Florence
12. Rome
13. Naples

Italy in the early sixteenth century

in the south of the peninsula. The House of Valois also laid claim to the kingdom and in recent decades had used force in attempting to make good their claim. Milan was a dynastic as well as a strategic bone of contention. Technically it fell under the authority of the Holy Roman Emperor, but the Valois dynasty possessed a claim to the duchy. In 1515 France seized the city of Milan. In 1516 Charles, as the new Spanish monarch, made peace with the French in the Treaty of Noyon. He recognised French rule over Milan. However, for Charles and his advisers the long-term loss of Milan was unthinkable. His family's long-standing claim to rule Milan as part of the Empire had been flouted. When Charles himself became Emperor in 1519 Milan provided an important gateway connecting the Empire with his lands in the south of Italy. It also provided a vital centre of communications linking together Spain, the Netherlands and Austria.

b) The Habsburg–Valois Wars, 1521–9

Between 1521 and 1529 Charles found himself almost continuously at war with France. What, then, triggered off this first phase of the Habsburg–Valois conflict under Charles V? In the Treaty of Noyon Charles had, in addition to sacrificing Milan, promised to return Navarre to France (see map, page 23). It had been seized by Charles' grandfather, Ferdinand of Aragon. However, Charles continued to postpone the restoration of Navarre, recognising the damage it would do to his standing among his Spanish subjects. By 1520 rumours of a French attack on Navarre were rife. In the meantime Charles was successful in concluding an alliance with Henry VIII of England. The French attacked in the summer of 1521, hoping to take advantage of the turmoil in Spain caused by the *Communeros* revolt. According to R. J. Knecht, a biographer of Francis I, 'It is unlikely that Francis intended these moves [on Navarre] to be the opening shots of a full-scale war with the emperor: he probably meant only to draw his attention away from Italy. But he seriously underestimated Charles' capacity to strike back.' The French enjoyed some initial success, capturing the city of Pamplona. However, once the *Communeros* revolt had been put down many of the former rebels joined Charles' army in driving the French out of Navarre. This victory confirmed Spain's possession of Navarre for the rest of Charles' reign.

The theatre of conflict now shifted to Italy. In 1521 Charles' closest adviser, the Burgundian Chièvres de Croy, died. He had advocated peaceful relations with France. His place was taken by Mercurino Gattinara, who now came to dominate Charles' political and strategic thinking. Gattinara promoted an aggressive imperial policy and, in particular, a forward policy in Italy. He immediately counselled the removal of French influence in the peninsula. Charles was persuaded and, after coming to an agreement with Pope Leo X, a joint Habsburg and papal army drove the French out of Milan in November 1521. The citizens of Milan welcomed back the pro-Habsburg duke, Francesco Sforza. At the same time, Charles seized Tournai from the French and incorporated it into the Netherlands. His success continued in 1522. A French attempt to retake Milan was repulsed. Then the French armies recklessly attacked a strong Habsburg position at Biocca, near Milan. The French forces were defeated in battle and other French garrisons in the north of Italy soon surrendered. Charles now held Milan securely and had gained control of northern Italy. Gattinara's advice appeared to be paying handsome dividends. Charles' confidence was such that he decided to carry the offensive to France itself.

The prospect of a successful invasion of France was unexpectedly assisted when the powerful French noble, the duke of Bourbon, abandoned his king and agreed to lead Habsburg troops against him. Bourbon was in dispute with Francis over his family lands and decided that a Habsburg victory over France was the best way of securing his future. In addition, the English alliance was now bearing fruit. Henry VIII promised to march his armies from Calais, under English occupation, to attack Paris. So, in the summer of 1523 France came under triple attack; from the English in the north and from Bourbon and the Habsburgs in the south. The situation seemed critical for the French king. However, the allied campaigns went badly. The English advance on Paris was half-hearted and Henry was glad to call it off when he heard that the offensives of his allies in the south were making little progress. An attempt to capture the Mediterranean port of Marseilles, for example, ended in ignominious retreat. By the end of the year it was obvious that attacks on France by an ill-co-ordinated alliance would achieve little. This greatly boosted French morale and Francis was able to retaliate with a military and diplomatic counter-offensive which nearly undid Charles successes hitherto. A new pope, Clement VII, was concerned about Habsburg dominance in Italy and its attendant threat to papal independence. He therefore brought Venice and Florence into an alliance with France. French armies crossed into Lombardy and, once again, Milan fell to them. Other French forces penetrated as far as Naples in the south. Charles was devastated by this sudden reversal of fortunes and appeared to lose his will to continue the fight. He recorded his thoughts thus:

1 When I sat down to think about my position, I saw that the first thing at which I must aim and the best that God could send me, was peace. Peace is beautiful to talk of but difficult to have, for as everyone knows it cannot be had without the enemy's consent. I
5 must therefore make great efforts – and that, too, is easier said than done. However much I scrape and save it is often difficult for me to find the necessary means.

A successful war may help me. But I cannot support my army

let alone increase it, if that should be necessary. Naples did not
10 provide the money I hoped for; that kingdom will have to manage
for itself if it is attacked. All sources of revenue here in Spain are
daily tapped without result; at this present moment it looks as if
nothing whatever could be raised. The king of England does not
help me as a true friend should; he does not even help me to the
15 extent of his obligations. My friends have forsaken me in my evil
hour; all are equally determined to prevent me from growing
more powerful and to keep me in my present distressed state.

However, Charles' fortunes were soon to revive. Early in 1525 his
forces in the city of Pavia, near Milan, put up an impressive resistance
to a French siege. Soon a relieving force from Germany descended on
the French outside the city. When Francis decided to confront these
forces in open battle the French were crushingly defeated. According to
some contemporary reports, Francis was trapped under his horse and it
was some time before the Habsburg troops identified him. Charles'
victory at the Battle of Pavia was his most decisive yet. The King of
France was his prisoner and France's best soldiery was slaughtered.
Italy, and Milan in particular, returned to Habsburg control. Charles
received the news of Pavia with dignity. He forbad wild rejoicing and,
instead, arranged for prayers of thanksgiving.

* Charles now had to decide what to do with the French king, and
what sort of settlement he should impose upon him. Francis was
escorted back to Spain, where Charles resolved to keep him hostage.
Charles had to judge how far he could push the French in their hour of
weakness. Such a judgement was of great long-term significance, as
Charles' viceroy in Naples pointed out:

> God sends to every man in the course of his life a good crop. If he
> does not harvest it well, he loses the opportunity forever.

Charles' brother Ferdinand and Henry VIII of England joined those
who advocated a harsh settlement. They recommended the sacking of
France and its partition between Charles and his allies. 'Now is the
time' declared Henry, 'for the Emperor and myself to devise means of
getting full satisfaction from France. Not an hour is to be lost.' Charles
rejected such draconian measures. His personal sense of honour
dictated otherwise and he was suspicious of Henry VIII's intentions.
His ultimate objective was to assert the legal claims of his family, not
territorial expansion, and therefore he suspended hostilities and concentrated on negotiating with the French from a position of strength.
Considerable progress was made. The French agreed to renounce their
claims to Flanders, Artois and Tournai. However, the sticking point

See Preface for explanation of * symbol.

was Burgundy. Charles insisted on the recovery of his ancestral lands. This would be a great boost to his dynastic pride and to his international reputation. Francis, on the other hand, could hardly retain any credibility if he sacrificed what was now, to all intents and purposes, an integral part of his kingdom. However, the French were not really in a position to bargain. The Treaty of Madrid (January 1526) gave Francis his freedom, but only at the cost of abandoning Burgundy. The treaty also provided for the marriage of Francis to Charles' sister, Eleonore, and for French participation in a crusade against the Ottoman Empire. Finally, Francis's two sons were to be kept hostage in Spain until the fulfilment of his treaty obligations. But what assurances did Charles have that Francis would observe the treaty, apart from the custody of the king's children? He had only Francis's word as a Christian knight. Charles was surely naive in believing that this was sufficient. In fact, in Madrid Francis had already signed a secret vow declaring that, as he had signed under duress, the treaty was invalid. Charles had been duped, and Francis was prepared to abandon his sons for the present in the hope of negotiating their release at a later date. Thus Charles failed to exploit his victory at Pavia, and it can be contended that he was left with the worst of both worlds. The Treaty of Madrid was now worthless, whilst Francis was further embittered and anxious for revenge.

When Francis returned to Paris, the Treaty of Madrid was declared null and void and the king vowed to continue his struggle against the Habsburgs. Charles soon faced a formidable alliance of opponents, all resentful at his recent triumphs. Firstly, Francis formed an alliance with the Ottomans, who agreed to launch an attack on Habsburg Austria from the Balkans. In England Henry VIII perceived the danger of a Habsburg colossus in Europe after the defeat of the one European power, France, capable of curbing Charles' ambitions. In Italy the papacy and the city-states began to see that the implication of Pavia was a diminution of their own independence in the face of Habsburg supremacy in the peninsula. Francis understood this and portrayed himself as a champion of Italian liberty. Therefore, in May 1526 Francis joined with the papacy, Venice, Florence and the now ousted Duke of Milan in an anti-Habsburg alliance, the League of Cognac, towards which the good wishes of Henry VIII were secured. The alliance's aim was to liberate Italy from Habsburg domination. Charles was distressed by the treachery which surrounded him, and in August 1526 he gave vent to his feelings before a French diplomat:

1 Had your king kept his word we should have been spared this. I
  will take no money from him, not even from his children. He has
  cheated me; he has acted neither as a knight nor as a nobleman,
  but basely. I demand that if he cannot fulfil his treaty, the Most
5 Christian King should keep his word or become my prisoner

again. It would be better for us to fight out this quarrel hand to hand than to shed so much Christian blood.

* The conflict which followed the formation of the League of Cognac lasted until the Peace of Cambrai in August 1529. At first it was something of a phoney war, with Francis reluctant to commit French troops so soon after his defeat at Pavia. The first drama of the war came in May 1527, when Habsburg troops stormed the city of Rome in the notorious 'Sack of Rome'. Charles had permitted his army garrisoned in Milan to be used against papal troops who were engaged against one of his Italian allies. Under the leadership of the Duke of Bourbon, and without Charles' approval, the Habsburg army marched on Rome. Bourbon died in the assault of the city, but it was successfully stormed on 6 May 1527. When the leaderless and unpaid troops, including German Protestants, conducted a week-long orgy of murder, rape and pillaging, Christian Europe was horrified. The Pope fled the city but was soon taken prisoner by Habsburg forces. Charles was genuinely dismayed by these events, but he was not prepared to admit personal responsibility. Instead, he mounted a propaganda campaign to convince Western Europe that the real blame lay with his enemies – the Pope and the King of France in particular – who were so determined to disturb the peace of Christendom. To Henry VIII he privately confessed that 'we have felt great pain and shame for the offence given to the Holy See, indeed we would have preferred not to win than to be left with such a victory.'

For Charles the consequences of the Sack of Rome were mixed. Late in 1527 he released the captive Pope, but Clement had been severely chastened and he was henceforth more reluctant to betray Charles. On the other hand, it helped prompt Henry VIII to align himself more openly with the anti-Habsburg front in Europe. He now wished to divorce Charles' aunt, Catherine of Aragon, and feared that a revival of Habsburg influence in Europe, and in Rome in particular, would be used to check his plans. In 1528 England and France jointly declared war on Charles, and English money was sent to aid the French campaigns in Italy. At first the war went well for the French and, although they failed to take Milan, French troops marched to challenge Habsburg control of Naples. Victory seemed within their grasp. The city of Naples was besieged by a large French army and blockaded at sea by a Genoese fleet, commanded by the Genoese admiral and statesman, Andrea Doria. However, Habsburg diplomacy saved the day. Doria was growing disillusioned with his French masters and Charles' agents persuaded him to desert the French and join the Habsburgs. This was a major coup for Charles. From now on he had the substantial Genoese fleet at his disposal in the Mediterranean and access to loans from Genoese bankers. More immediately, the blockade of Naples was lifted and the city was reinforced from Spain and Sicily.

The French, now afflicted by plague, raised the siege and retreated northwards. The Habsburg–Valois struggle in Italy returned to a stalemate. However, in June 1529 the French, once again, tried to take Milan. Their armies were defeated decisively at the Battle of Landriano, which marked the end of the long years of war. Charles was master of Italy again, and it remained only to attempt another peace treaty with the defeated French.

The Peace of Cambrai was signed in August 1529, and brought to a close nearly a decade of conflict. Both sides now realised that a continuation of war would put an intolerable strain upon their resources. Charles was afforded a second opportunity to make peace from a position of strength. His aunt, Margaret of Austria, had already negotiated a truce with England. She met the French queen-mother, Louise of Savoy, and it did not take the two women long to conclude a treaty. The treaty became known as 'the Ladies Peace'. The French renounced their claims to Naples, Flanders, Artois and Tournai. They also surrendered their claim to Milan, where a pro-Habsburg member of the Sforza family was restored. Preparations were made for the long-postponed marriage of Francis to Charles' sister, Eleonore, which took place the following year. The French promised to pay Charles 300,000 ducats for the release of the two royal sons from captivity in Spain. Francis pledged to join Charles in a crusade against his former ally, the Ottoman Sultan. Therefore the Peace of Cambrai largely duplicated the Treaty of Madrid in 1526, although Charles now relinquished his claim to his ancestral Burgundian lands. For Francis the terms of the Peace of Cambrai were punitive and contemporaries expressed surprise that he accepted it; but Charles came out of it extremely well. He was anxious to secure a period of peace, and was willing to sacrifice Burgundy to this end. Otherwise, he got everything he wanted and, above all, he secured Habsburg mastery in Italy. The peace terminated the most continuous and bloody chapter in the Habsburg–Valois struggle.

c) The Habsburg–Valois Wars, 1529–44

It was not long before it became apparent that the Peace of Cambrai had not totally resolved Habsburg–Valois differences. Francis felt dishonoured and was anxious to restore some sort of balance of power between France and the Habsburg empire. Above all, he wished to recover Milan. At first, he resorted to diplomatic intrigue. Approaches were made to Henry VIII and to Charles' Protestant opponents in Germany. Pope Clement VII continued to chafe at Habsburg dominance in Italy. In 1533 he agreed to the marriage of his niece, Catherine de Medici, to Francis's eldest son, the future Henry II. When Charles captured the north African city of Tunis in 1535 he uncovered documentary evidence that Francis was again conspiring with the Ottoman Sultan.

However, it was Charles' actions which sparked off a resumption of war. Late in 1535 the last of the Sforzas died and Charles decided to take formal possession of the duchy of Milan. This was a slap in the face to Francis, who considered Charles to be violating the agreement he had entered into at Cambrai. In 1536 Francis, in retaliation, ordered his troops into Piedmont and Savoy, from where he was better able to launch an attack on Milan. His troops captured the city of Turin, in Piedmont (Piedmont and Savoy were held by the French until 1559). Charles denounced French belligerency. In a letter to his wife he revealed guarded optimism about the conflict to come:

> I believe this war will be like the last one, with France winning some points at the beginning but, with the help of God, being defeated in the end by our troops.

Charles' predictions were not very accurate. In fact, neither side achieved any notable victories. A French attack on Milan was driven back, but Habsburg forces were unable to dislodge the French from Turin. Next, Charles led an army of 60,000 into Provence in the south-eastern corner of France. French resistance was furious. Charles failed to take his next objective, the port of Marseilles, and reluctantly ordered a retreat. By 1538 it was obvious that a deadlock had been reached. Both sides had seriously drained their resources, and the Pope urged a truce. Charles' wife, Empress Isabella, and his sister Eleonore (now the French queen) did likewise. Charles, himself, was beginning to think more about a crusade against the Muslim forces in the Mediterranean. In the spring of 1538 Charles and Francis met at Nice to begin negotiations, but Francis proved to be obdurate and only the intervention of the Pope persuaded him to moderate his unrealistic demands. Finally, Charles and Francis signed a ten-year truce at Aigues-Mortes, near Nice. France was left in temporary possession of Savoy and Piedmont and the problem of the future of Milan was shelved, at Charles' insistence, for he had little to lose from the *status quo*. The two monarchs declared their intention to mount a crusade against the Ottomans. In retrospect, it can be seen that the Treaty of Nice was a somewhat makeshift arrangement. The root causes of Habsburg-Valois conflict, especially the fate of Milan, were left unresolved.

[*In 1540 Charles brought Milan more tightly within the Habsburg orbit by formally investing his son Philip with the duchy.]This strengthened the French king's resentment against Habsburg predominance in Europe. Any difficulty Charles was to face would be France's opportunity. In 1541 Charles' expedition to rid Algiers of Muslim pirates failed disastrously. He also continued to face daunting religious difficulties in Germany. Francis was provided with a useful pretext for war in 1541 when two of his envoys, *en route* to secret negotiations with the Ottoman Sultan, were murdered in the Habsburg-controlled duchy of Milan. He blamed Charles, without any evidence of his complicity, calling the murders 'an injury so great, so detestable and so strange to those who bear the title and quality of prince that it cannot in any way be forgiven, suffered or endured'. In 1542 he declared war on Charles, despite peace pleas from the Pope and Charles' promise to set up an enquiry into the killings. The war lasted from 1542 to 1544. It was a muddled affair which shifted from one front to another and ended in another stalemate. In 1542 the French captured Nice from Charles' ally, the duke of Savoy, in a combined operation with an Ottoman fleet. They also took the frontier fortress of Luxemburg, in alliance with the Duke of Cleves, a German Protestant prince. In Piedmont, Charles' imperial army was defeated at Ceresole, but the French were unable to follow up their victory with an assault on Milan. Charles' forces succeeded in beating off a French attack on Catalonia, in northern Spain. A French offensive against the Netherlands was also checked. Furthermore, Charles was gaining the upper-hand in international diplomacy. Henry VIII agreed to support him, as Anglo-French relations deteriorated and as he saw the opportunity to take advantage of French weakness in time of war. Moreover, the Franco-Ottoman alliance shocked many in Christendom. In Germany, for example, both Protestant and Catholic gave generously to the Emperor to assist his fight against the unholy alliance of France and Islam. In 1544 Charles embarked on an invasion of France in conjunction with Henry VIII. The imperial army came within striking distance of Paris. However, the English again proved to be unreliable allies. Instead of reinforcing his ally, Henry concentrated on capturing Boulogne for himself. Meanwhile, the Habsburg offensive began to disintegrate when Charles was unable to pay his troops. By the autumn of 1544 both sides were nearing exhaustion. A truce with the Habsburgs would enable the French king to protect Boulogne from English attack. Charles was becoming anxious to devote more of his resources to settling the religious conflict in Germany. Francis hinted to Charles that, if a truce were achieved, he would be able to help him in Germany. Therefore, it was not difficult to conclude a treaty at Crépy in September 1544. In territorial terms, the Peace of Crépy replicated the Treaty of Nice of 1538, with Charles maintaining his grip on Italy. In dynastic matters, Francis's younger son was to marry a Habsburg princess, although his death the next year put an end to the plan (see page 54). Charles also gained in wider political terms. The end of the Franco-Ottoman alliance, which followed the treaty, was a great relief to the Emperor. More significantly, the French agreed to help Charles in his efforts to heal religious divisions in Germany. Charles' victory over the German Protestants at the Battle of Mühlberg (see page 95) was helped by the French policy of non-intervention arising from Crépy.

b) The Habsburg–Valois Wars, 1544–59

The Peace of Crépy of 1544 was very much a peace of exhaustion. It was unpopular in France and the failure of its marriage provisions removed one of the foundations of the peace. As the grievances of the French were still unmet, it was likely that they would exploit any of Charles' future difficulties to redress them. In 1547, following his dramatic victory over the German Protestants at Mühlberg, Charles' power and prestige in Europe were at their height. Yet, as the decade came to a close, his success in Germany began to crumble when Catholic and Protestant princes refused to lend him their support (see page 96). During this period he also became embroiled in family arguments over the succession to his many territories. In 1551 his position was further weakened when his truce with the Sultan came to an end. Tripoli, in north Africa, was immediately lost to an Ottoman attack. Meanwhile, in France, Francis I had died in March 1547 and had been succeeded by his son Henry II. Henry had spent three years in Habsburg captivity in Spain and was, naturally, not well-disposed toward Charles. On the other hand, the new king was anxious to establish his authority at home. Foreign adventures were at first eschewed, and peace was maintained until the early 1550s. Some historians have argued that Henry was less interested in combatting the Habsburgs in Italy than in challenging their power in northern Europe. This is unlikely. Nevertheless, when opportunities arose for him to do harm to the Habsburgs outside Italy he seized them eagerly. In January 1552 he concluded the Treaty of Chambord with the German Protestants. In it he promised to aid their struggle against the Habsburgs in Germany. They, in return, promised to give him possession of the three important imperial bishoprics bordering France – Metz, Toul and Verdun. A Habsburg–Valois war inevitably ensued and it was to last beyond Charles' abdication and death.

The wider international developments which attended this phase of the Habsburg–Valois wars were, as usual, very important. Charles' position in Germany deteriorated; Protestant opposition became so formidable that he had to flee the country in May 1552 and hand over authority to his brother Ferdinand. It was not long before events in Italy were also ominous. When Pope Paul IV was elected in 1555 he adopted a fiercely anti-Habsburg policy. The papacy allied with France, and the Pope encouraged Henry II to attempt to seize Naples from the Habsburgs. However, the subsequent French invasion failed and there were other promising straws in the wind for Charles. In England, Charles' cousin, Mary Tudor, succeeded to the throne in 1553. In 1554 the Anglo-Habsburg relationship was sealed when Mary married Charles' son, Philip. Having England as an ally was a great strategic advantage. France was now even more effectively encircled and English seapower could guarantee Charles' maritime lines of communication between Spain and the Netherlands.

The main military confrontations between the Habsburgs and the French took place between 1552 and 1554 in the Netherlands and at the fortress of Metz, occupied by the French in 1552. The fortress was of vital strategic importance as, in French hands, it cut the Habsburg lines of communication between the Empire and the Netherlands. Late in 1552 Charles marched a massive imperial army to the fortress. He was disappointed that, because of illness, he was not able to lead his troops personally in the assault. The French put up a skilled defence and Charles was compelled to raise the siege in January 1553. His failure to regain Metz marked a turning-point in this phase of the Habsburg–Valois wars. He was plunged into deep despair. In a letter written to Philip during the closing stages of the siege he complained of his physical suffering from gout, and he recognised that the campaign against the French was driving him into hopeless financial insolvency. For the next month he suffered from insomnia and depression. The French campaign against the Netherlands in 1553 was bloody and devastating. There were times when it looked as if the Low Countries would fall to the invading armies. Charles, in his last military campaign, helped organise successful resistance. However, he had realised after Metz that a decisive victory over the French was beyond him. This realisation marks the beginning of a serious loss of will, which was to lead to his abdication in 1555.

After Charles' abdication, Philip came to terms with the King of France in the Treaty of Vaucelles in February 1556. Nevertheless, war between the Houses of Habsburg and Valois continued intermittently until 1559. In his retirement at Yuste, Charles nurtured a desire for revenge against the French. He urged Spain and the Netherlands to provide sufficient resources to Philip to enable him to continue the struggle and he pressed Philip to establish a reputation as a war leader. However, other circumstances encouraged a more peaceful resolution of the conflict. The division of Charles' empire between Philip and Ferdinand relaxed French fears of encirclement. A further reduction in tension resulted from the death of Philip's wife, Mary Tudor, in 1558. This ended the Anglo-Spanish alliance. However, it was the bankruptcies of both the French and the Spanish monarchies in 1557 which really made peace inevitable. After the long decades of war the resources of Philip and Henry could quite simply no longer support war. The result was the Treaty of Cateau-Cambrésis in 1559. This treaty marks the conclusion of the Habsburg–Valois conflict. In it the House of Valois renounced its claims to most of the territories disputed – Artois, Flanders, Tournai and Navarre. They returned Savoy to the pro-Habsburg Duke of Savoy. They retained only Burgundy and the fortresses of Metz, Toul and Verdun. In Italy, the treaty seemed to vindicate Charles' prolonged struggle to uphold his dynastic rights. Habsburg possession of Milan and Naples was confirmed. The entire peninsula was thereby left very much under Habsburg influence. The treaty also provided for the marriage of Philip II to Elizabeth, the daughter of Henry II. The provisions of the treaty largely survived until the middle of the next century and peace between the Houses of Habsburg and Valois lasted for almost 30 years.

e) Assessment

What, then, did the Houses of Habsburg and Valois gain, if anything, from their long wars? It should be borne in mind that in the sixteenth century war was not generally perceived in the same way that it is today. We tend to consider war as a tragedy or an evil in itself. In the sixteenth century it was considered by many as the natural 'sport' of kings and nobles, a contest in which knightly repute and booty were the prizes. War, therefore, enabled Charles and the Kings of France to bolster their reputations as soldier-kings and provide an outlet for the restless energies of their nobles. The French enjoyed some limited successes. In the 1520s they prevented Charles from realising his ambition of regaining Burgundy. In addition, some historians argue that the acquisition of the strategically important bishoprics of Metz, Toul and Verdun was a gain of long-term significance for the French. However, Charles was undoubtedly more successful in asserting his territorial and dynastic rights. Outside Italy, Navarre, Flanders, Artois, Tournai and Cambrai were consolidated within the Habsburg empire. In Italy he could hardly have hoped for more. His claim to Naples was successfully defended, but it was the maintenance of Habsburg control of Milan that was the Emperor's greatest success. He invested great dynastic pride in Milan and it provided a vital centre of communication within the Habsburg empire. From the time of Charles V the French effectively abandoned their dynastic and strategic ambitions in Italy. Charles, on the other hand, ensured his dynasty's future in the peninsula. Italy was soon to become, in effect, a Spanish colony. This, in turn, helped to pave the way for a century of Spanish hegemony in Europe as a whole.

However, both sides paid a heavy price for the decades of war. The French were less able to support such a lengthy conflict. The results were very high levels of taxation for the French people and enormous royal debts. Thus some historians argue that the prolonged period of monarchical weakness, political instability and civil war which followed the Habsburg–Valois wars originated, in part, in the damage inflicted upon France by the costs of the wars. Charles had more resources at his disposal. The wealth of the New World, the Netherlands and Castile was milked to finance his wars against the French. However, the financial strains on the Habsburgs were also enormous. Charles bequeathed his son Philip a legacy of debt which forced him into bankruptcy as early as 1557. But Charles' greatest regret was his failure to secure a lasting peace with France. His determination to assert his dynastic rights could not be reconciled with France's strategic and territorial aspirations. Thus Habsburg–Valois attempts at peace-making were doomed to failure. France never accepted Charles' terms for peace, except out of short-term expediency. Sooner or later, the House of Valois re-opened hostilities in the hope of overturning Habsburg dominance in Europe. Charles, on the other hand, genuinely wished to secure peace amongst the dynasties of Christendom in order to be able to devote more of his resources to his other priorities – ending the religious schism in Germany and lauching a Christian offensive against Islam. The Habsburg–Valois wars, more than anything else, frustrated these ambitions. Not only did the French provide a constant distraction for the Emperor, but they also actively aided his German and Muslim opponents.

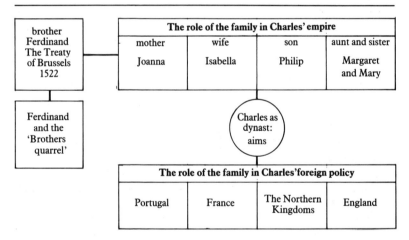

Summary – The Family

The Habsburg–Valois Rivalry

Date	Military	Diplomatic
1516		Treaty of Noyon
1521	French attack Navarre	Anglo-Habsburg alliance
	Habsburgs capture Milan and Tournai	Habsburg alliance with Pope Paul X
1522	Battle of Biocca	
1523	Habsburgs, England and Bourbon attack France	Duke of Bourbon allies with Habsburgs Election of Pope Clement VII

Date	Military	Diplomatic
1524	French recapture Milan	Pope allies with French
1525	Battle of Pavia	
1526		Treaty of Madrid
		League of Cognac
1527	Sack of Rome	
1528	French besiege Naples	France and England declare war on Habsburgs
		Admiral Doria defects to Habsburgs
1529	Battle of Landriano	Peace of Cambrai
1535		Charles takes formal possession of Madrid
1536	French capture Turin	First alliance between
	Charles invades France	French and Ottomans
1538		'Ten Year' truce at Treaty of Nice
1540		Philip invested with Milan
1541		French envoys murdered
1542	French capture Nice and fortress of Luxemburg	
	Battle of Ceresole	
	French attack Catalonia and Netherlands	
1543		Anglo-Habsburg alliance
1544	England and Habsburgs invade France	Peace of Crépy and end of Franco-Ottoman alliance
1547		Charles triumphant in Germany. Death of Francis I and succession of Henry II
1552	Henry II captures Metz, Toul and Verdun	Treaty of Chambord and Protestant revolt in Germany
1553	Charles raises siege of Metz	
	French attack Netherlands	
1554	Charles' last military campaign	Philip marries Mary Tudor
1555	French attack Naples	Election of Pope Paul IV, who allies with France
1556		Treaty of Vaucelles
1559		Treaty of Cateau-Cambrésis

Making notes on 'Charles the Dynast'

1 The Family
As you will note in the 'Answering Essay Questions' section below, the role of Charles' family does not, as a rule, appear on its own in essay questions. Therefore it is important not to get 'bogged down' in attempting to document every detail of his family policy. The important tasks are a) to acquire an understanding of what his dynastic objectives were, and b) to be able to illustrate the broad lines of his policy with appropriate evidence from this section. Your notes can afford to be briefer than those on 'Charles the Ruler', and the following headings and questions should provide a suitable framework.
1.1.   In what ways was Charles a dynast?
1.2.   What roles did Charles allocate to members of his family? Deal with each separately and decide what degree of success he enjoyed in each case – a) his brother Ferdinand b) his mother Joanna c) his wife Isabella d) his son Philip e) Margaret and Mary, his regents in the Netherlands.
1.3.   Dynastic Foreign Policy
1.3.1. How successfully did Charles cement ties between his own family and the Portuguese House of Avis?
1.3.2. How far did Charles achieve his dynastic aims in relation to France?
1.3.3. Why did Charles not provide more active support for his relatives in the northern kingdoms?
1.3.4. Why were Charles' ties with the Tudor dynasty in England likely to be close?
1.3.5. Why did Charles oppose Henry VIII's proposed divorce from Catherine of Aragon and what steps did he take to this end?
1.3.6. In what ways were Charles' hopes of securing Mary Tudor's succession frustrated by Henry VIII's actions?
1.3.7. Why did Charles not provide more active support for Mary Tudor's claims to the English throne?
1.3.8. Account for the gradual improvement in Anglo-Habsburg relations from 1536.
1.4.   The Succession to Charles
1.4.1. Why did Charles change his mind about the imperial succession in the later 1540s?
1.4.2. What was agreed upon at the Augsburg discussions and what obstacles were there to implementing the agreements?
1.4.3. Account for the deterioration of family relations after the Augsburg discussions.
1.4.4. Why did Charles' plans for the imperial succession fail?
1.5.   To what extent did dynastic principles guide Charles' actions and how successful was he in applying them?

2 The Habsburg–Valois Rivalry

When you are taking notes on this topic do not become too immersed in the purely military aspects of the conflict. You are not studying 'military history' as such. You only require a very brief summary of the major campaigns and battles. However, it will be useful to gather evidence which helps to explain why neither side was able to achieve a decisive military victory. Other important themes to bear in mind as you take notes are:

a) What were Charles' aims and objectives?
b) What were the aims and objectives of Francis I and Henry II?
c) Assess the attempts at peace-making and why they failed so frequently.
d) How important were the diplomatic developments which accompanied the conflict?

2.1.   What were the causes of the conflict?
2.2.   The Habsburg–Valois Wars, 1521–9.
2.2.1. What triggered off the conflict? How successful was Charles in it and what was the significance of the Battle of Pavia?
2.2.2. What did Charles aim to achieve from the Treaty of Madrid and why was he not successful?
2.2.3. Why was the League of Cognac formed?
2.2.4. What was the significance of the 'Sack of Rome' and what successes did Charles enjoy after it?
2.2.5. What were Charles' aims at the Peace of Cambrai and how successful was he in achieving them?
2.3.   The Habsburg–Valois Wars, 1529–44.
2.3.1. What triggered off the conflict in 1536?
2.3.2. Why did the conflict end in a truce in 1538 and what did Charles gain from the truce?
2.3.3. What triggered off the conflict in 1542 and how successful was Charles in it?
2.3.4. Why did both sides enter into the Peace of Crépy in 1544 and what did Charles achieve by it?
2.4.   The Habsburg–Valois Wars, 1544–59.
2.4.1. In what ways was Charles' position weakened between 1547 and 1552 and what triggered off conflict in 1552?
2.4.2. What international developments accompanied this phase of the conflict?
2.4.3. How successful was Charles in this phase of the conflict?
2.4.4. Why did both sides enter into the Treaty of Cateau-Cambrésis and how well did the Habsburgs come out of it?
2.5.   Assessment: Which side do you think derived the greatest benefit from the Habsburg–Valois rivalry?

Answering essay questions on 'Charles the Dynast'

Historical writings on Charles V do not in general deal with the role of his family as a distinct and separate theme. Therefore examiners have not felt it appropriate to set questions dealing exclusively with this aspect of his reign. However the section on 'The Family' provides useful information for answering questions such as:

1. What methods did Charles V employ to govern his different dominions, and how successful were they?

In addition, the role of the Habsburg family may be relevant to broader questions on Charles' foreign policy. Questions on foreign policy invariably concentrate on the Habsburg–Valois rivalry, but some allow for a consideration of Charles' relations with other countries as well. The information you have from this chapter on Charles' dynastic relations with Portugal, the northern kingdoms and England (as well as France) would be relevant in such cases. In which of these two questions would they be relevant?

2. To what extent was Charles V's greatest success in foreign policy achieved in Italy?
3. Why did Charles V experience such prolonged conflict with Francis I in Italy?

Questions on the Habsburg–Valois rivalry are very common. However, bear in mind that that they can be combined with the Italian Wars which preceded the reign of Charles V. Bear in mind, also, that this chapter deals with the Habsburg–Valois rivalry largely from the Habsburg point of view. For more general questions on the conflict it would be useful to have more evidence on the roles of the French kings (see *France: Renaissance, Religion and Recovery* by Martyn Rady, in this series). The most common questions on the Habsburg–Valois rivalry are of two broad types. The first focuses on the causes of the conflict and on the aims and objectives of the protagonists. for example:

4. Account for the long periods of conflict between Charles V and Francis I.
5. To what extent was it the importance that Francis I and Charles V attached to Italy that explains the Habsburg–Valois rivalry?
6. Why was Charles V involved in such prolonged conflict with the kings of France?

It is very important not to write a narrative 'story' of the Habsburg–Valois rivalry in responding to these questions. However, you can structure your answer around the chronological units in this chapter. For example, plan an answer to question 5, using the following guidance:

a) Introduction: What range of factors, in addition to Italy, can be identified which help to explain the Habsburg–Valois rivalry?
b) For each period (1521–9, 1529–44 and 1544–59) assess the importance of Italy, relative to other factors (some periods might well be dealt with in more than one paragraph).
c) Conclusion: On the basis of your evidence in b), how important was Italy in comparison with other factors?

The second type of question on the Habsburg–Valois rivalry focuses on the results and consequences of the conflict. For example:

7. 'A long struggle which achieved nothing.' How apt is this as a description of Charles V's conflict with the Kings of France?
8. To what extent was Charles V's success in Italy his only one in the Habsburg–Valois conflict?

The answers to these questions can be structured like those above on the causes of the rivalry. For example, plan an answer to question 8, using the following guidance:

a) Introduction: What successes are commonly attributed to Charles in the Habsburg–Valois rivalry?
b) For each period (1521–9, 1529–44 and 1544–59) assess Charles' successes, noting particularly which proved to be enduring (again, some periods might well be dealt with in more than one paragraph).
c) Conclusion: On the basis of your evidence in b) do you consider that there were other significant successes, besides Italy?

Finally, the dynastic aspects of Charles' reign are relevant to general questions on his aims and objectives, and the degree to which he achieved them. For example:

9. What were the aims and ambitions of Charles V, and how far did he fulfil them?

Practise condensing your material on 'Charles the Dynast' so as to contribute only a paragraph or two in answer to a question as broad in scope as this.

Source-based questions on 'Charles the Dynast'

1 The 'Brothers' Quarrel'
Read the Augsburg memorandum on page 61, and answer the following questions:
a) What is the single most important attribute of the successor to the imperial throne, according to the memorandum? (*1 mark*)

b) Explain in your own words what the author perceives to be the advantages and disadvantages of Philip's succession. *(4 marks)*
c) What evidence does the memorandum contain of the dynastic pride of the Habsburgs? *(2 marks)*
d) Is it possible to detect whether the author favours Ferdinand or Philip? Give your reasons. *(3 marks)*

2 Dividing the empire

Examine the painting of Charles dividing his empire on page 60. Ferdinand is standing to his right, Philip to his left. Answer the following questions:
a) What detail does the artist include to show that Charles is resigning his offices? *(1 mark)*
b) What techniques does the artist employ in his portrayal of Charles, Ferdinand and Philip, and what impression do you think he is trying to convey about each character? Give reasons to support your answer. *(9 marks)*
c) From your own knowledge, to what extent does the artist accurately portray the way in which Charles' empire was divided at the end of his reign? *(5 marks)*

3 Charles on the Habsburg–Valois conflict

Study the two extracts on pages 67–8 and 69–70, in which Charles reveals his thoughts about the conflict with France and answer the following questions:
a) What evidence is there in the second extract on pages 69–70 of the influence of the ideals of chivalry on Charles? *(2 marks)*
b) What do the two extracts reveal about the reasons for Charles' reluctance to engage in war with France? *(4 marks)*
c) How does the tone of Charles' public utterances on pages 69–70 differ from that in his private record on pages 67–8? *(4 marks)*
d) From the evidence of both extracts, how would you describe Charles' state of mind in the mid-1520s? *(5 marks)*

CHAPTER 4

Charles the Defender of the Faith

Much of Charles V's life was spent trying to combat critics of the Catholic Church within Europe and opposing Muslim powers who threatened Europe from outside. Why, then, did Charles attach so much importance to upholding the authority of the 'universal' Catholic Church? As we have seen (page 4), in his Burgundian boyhood Charles had absorbed a keen Catholic devoutness and a reverence for the Church. Later, Spanish influences were strong upon him when he became King of Spain. From the Spanish Charles assimilated something of their Catholic enthusiasm and strict devotion to Church belief and ritual. His responsibility for defending the established Church arose also from his position as Holy Roman Emperor. By long tradition this title conferred on its holder the responsibility for providing protection for the Catholic Church. This responsibility was made clear at Charles' coronation as Holy Roman Emperor at Aachen in 1519. In a deeply religious ceremony, Charles had to swear to uphold the Catholic faith, to protect the Church and to show reverence to the supreme authority of the Pope. Charles' acute consciousness of his dynastic obligations also influenced his attitude towards the Church. As we have seen (page 48), he was determined to pass on to his successors intact those territories he had inherited from his ancestors. For Charles, such dynastic obligations took on a religious as well as territorial meaning. He felt duty-bound to protect and preserve the Church of his forbears, as well as their lands. This he made clear in a speech to the German Diet at Worms in 1521:

> 1 You know that I am born of the most Christian Emperors of the noble German nation, and of the Catholic Kings of Spain, the Archdukes of Austria, the Dukes of Burgundy, who were all to the death true sons of the Roman Church, defenders of the
> 5 Catholic Faith, of the sacred customs, decrees, and uses of its worship, who have bequeathed all this to me as my heritage, and according to whose example I have hitherto lived.

Moreover, it should be borne in mind that the Church was an integral part of the social and political hierarchy of early modern Europe. The common institutions of the Church, and the single faith it preached, had an important part to play in maintaining social order and political stability in Europe. To question the authority of the Church was to undermine not only established religious belief, but also the foundations of vested political interests in Europe. It did not escape the attention of rulers like Charles V that attacks upon the Church were often accompanied by social unrest and political strife. Finally, the unity of Christendom was particularly important to Charles V because of the external threat of Islam.

For centuries the most pressing challenge to Catholic Europe was not from internal dissent, but from Muslim powers which threatened in the Mediterranean and from the Ottoman Empire in the East. European hostility to the followers of the prophet Mohammed (the faith of Islam) was centuries old. Although European Crusades against Muslim powers in the Middle East had come to an end in the thirteenth century, Europeans still shared the religious and racial hatred of the 'Infidel' (literally the unfaithful). It was natural that Charles grew up to absorb such strongly anti-Islamic prejudices. Burgundians were particularly proud of their historic contributions to the Crusades against Islam. In his childhood Charles enjoyed playing Christians versus Muslims. It is recorded that he always played the Christian part and that he always won. Spain, too, had a particularly strong anti-Islamic tradition. From the eighth to the fifteenth centuries large parts of the country had been occupied by Muslim forces from north Africa (the Moors). The Christian re-conquest of Muslim Spain (the *Reconquista*) had fostered heroic legends of Christian valour and a deep-seated hostility to Islam. Some of this distinctly Spanish anti-Muslim enthusiasm is likely to have rubbed off on Charles after he became King of Spain. In addition, the Holy Roman Emperor was by tradition a figurehead of Christian defiance of the 'Infidel'. Charles' grandfather and predecessor as Emperor, Maximilian, prided himself on such a sense of mission. Charles, as always, was anxious to live up to family traditions.

1 The Protestant Challenge in Germany

a) Martin Luther, 1517–21

In October 1517 the German monk and professor, Martin Luther, launched an attack on the Church's sale of Indulgences in Germany. The sellers of Indulgences told people that the purchase of these documents would ensure God's forgiveness of their sins, and even the forgiveness of the sins of their deceased relatives. The Church had a complex theological justification for the sale of Indulgences, but the sale had clearly become a financial racket. Yet Luther's attack was not based upon the financial impropriety surrounding Indulgences, but on deeply held religious misgivings about them. Having entered the controversy over Indulgences, he now began to elaborate and publicise his religious beliefs. He believed that salvation depended on the faith of the Christian alone, and that 'good works', like the purchase of Indulgences, were a dangerous distraction from faith. Salvation was, therefore, a matter of the direct relation between the individual and God. He rejected the claims of the Church that it could bring mankind into contact with God through its rituals and he denounced the Pope's claim to represent God on earth as fraudulent. The Bible, and not the teachings of the Church, provided a true revelation of God's will. A more fundamental indictment of the authority of the Catholic Church would have been difficult to imagine.

Luther's message immediately elicited substantial support in Germany and by 1520 he was something of a national hero. There is an immense body of historical writing which seeks to explain the popularity of Luther's teachings. Here we can only delineate some of the more obvious factors. Many were undoubtedly inspired by Luther's simple message that the individual could achieve salvation without recourse to the elaborate and expensive mediation of the Church. Many Germans strongly resented the domination of the Church in Germany by an Italian hierarchy based in Rome. They also took offence at the Roman Church's financial impositions on Germany. It is unlikely that such a revolutionary message could have survived in other areas of Europe where centralised political authority was stronger. The fragmented nature of political control in Germany made dissent much harder to check. The death of Emperor Maximilian in 1519 and the election of a new and young emperor in the same year further weakened central authority in Germany. In addition, the papacy was slow to appreciate the seriousness of the situation. At first Pope Leo X urged Luther to recant. It was not until June 1520 that he threatened to excommunicate him. When Luther failed to show the slightest remorse the Pope finally pronounced Luther's excommunication in January 1521. At the same time he pressed the new Emperor, Charles V, to deal with his heretical subject.

Charles agreed publicly to condemn Luther's teachings and to forbid their printing and publication in Germany. However, he was in a delicate political position. Luther lived under the jurisdiction of Frederick, the Elector of Saxony, and he taught at the Elector's prized university at Wittenberg. Frederick was a particularly powerful German prince and Charles was fearful of antagonising him at so early a stage in his imperial career. In addition, he did not wish to give the impression to other German princes that he intended to govern the Empire without taking their opinions into account. Charles, therefore, accepted Frederick's conciliatory advice and called Luther (under a promise of safe conduct) to explain himself before a meeting of the Imperial Diet at Worms in April 1521. Charles hoped that Luther could be prevailed upon to recant, but instead, he gave a dramatic and inspiring defence of his teachings. Charles had hoped to bolster his own prestige by being the one to silence Luther; he was, therefore, extremely affronted by Luther's intransigence and he composed his own reply to Luther, which he addressed to the Diet:

1 A single monk, led astray by private judgement, has set himself

against the faith held by all Christians for a thousand years or more, and impudently concludes that all Christians up till now have erred. I have therefore resolved to stake upon this cause all
5 my dominions, my friends, my body and my blood, my life and my soul. For myself and you, sprung from the holy German nation, appointed by particular privilege defenders of the faith, it would be a serious disgrace, an eternal stain upon ourselves and posterity, if, in this our day, not only heresy, but its very
10 suspicions, were due to our neglect. After Luther's stiff-necked reply yesterday, I now repent that I have so long delayed proceedings against him and his false doctrines. I have now resolved never again, under any circumstances, to hear him. Under protection of his safe conduct he shall be escorted home,
15 but forbidden to preach and to seduce men with his evil doctrines and incite then to rebellion.

The Diet supported Charles and, in the Edict of Worms, declared Luther a heretic and an outlaw. Yet, despite all these grand-sounding statements, the consequences of the Diet of Worms were slight. Many of the princes who had endorsed the edict were sympathetic to much of Luther's criticism of the Roman Church. Hence, whilst in some parts of Germany the edict was implemented rigorously, in others it was largely ignored. Charles had too much of a sense of honour to apprehend Luther when he was under the promise of safe conduct. Luther therefore fled into the secret protection of the elector of Saxony. There he continued his propaganda against the Church, whilst his ideas continued to circulate in Germany.

b) The Years of Appeasement, 1521–41

For the next 20 years Lutheranism continued to grow in strength and to establish itself in many parts of Germany. Charles was largely absent from the Empire and, despite his deep and instinctive distaste for any manifestation of heresy, little was done actively to counteract the progress of Lutheranism. His approach was certainly patient and conciliatory, but it has also been interpreted by some historians as displaying weakness, uncertainty and vacillation.

During the 1520s support for Luther's teaching grew dramatically and his ideas spread among the peasantry. Popular support for Luther induced many of the German towns and cities to establish reformed churches based on his ideas. Several powerful princes abandoned Catholicism and embraced the new religion. The successful establishment of Lutheranism in parts of Germany was made possible by the large measure of independence enjoyed by the princes and the cities. Already it was clear that religion and politics were impossible to disentangle in the Empire; city and princely authorities felt strongly that the faith of the German people lay within their own jurisdiction, not that of the Emperor. The weakness of central authority in the Empire was further aggravated by Charles' absence from 1521 to 1530. His brother Ferdinand was given responsibility over German affairs, but he was often distracted by Ottoman advances in the east of Europe and by the need to look after his lands in Austria and Hungary. The Habsburg response to the rise of Lutheranism in the 1520s was hardly vigorous or sustained.

Charles hoped that diplomacy and negotiation would succeed in solving the religious divisions in the Empire. He recognised that the authority of the Emperor depended on the willing consent of his more powerful subjects. He needed German support for his wars against the French and the Ottomans. He did have some sympathy with the criticisms levelled by the Lutherans against the administration of the Roman Church. But, above all, he was committed to preserving a united and universal Church and therefore sought to bring the dissidents back into the Catholic fold. This he tried to achieve in two ways. Firstly, he aimed to arrange a meeting of a General Council of the Church. The idea of a General Council was not a new one. Previously, the leading ecclesiastical and political authorities of Christendom had met in such a council to discuss institutional and doctrinal problems in the Church. Secondly, Charles resorted to the Imperial Diet as a means of attaining a religious truce until such time as a General Council of the Church could meet and work out a reconciliation between Catholicism and Lutheranism. He planned to return to Germany in person and attend a meeting of the Imperial Diet at Speyer in 1526. However, other distractions forced him to cancel his visit and, instead, Ferdinand was instructed to bring the two sides together. At the Diet Ferdinand demanded that the Edict of Worms against Lutheranism be implemented throughout the Empire. However, he held out an olive branch to the Lutherans by promising that a final verdict on their grievances might await a meeting of a General Council of the Church. This was the first of the Habsburgs' many concessions to the Lutheran opposition in Germany. However, the Diet ignored imperial demands and both Lutherans and Catholics at the Diet passed a resolution stating 'that each one should so live, govern and conduct himself as he hopes and trusts to answer it to God and to his imperial majesty'. What this meant in practice was that the German princes and towns should decide on matters of faith within their own territorial jurisdiction. This was a complete reversal of the Edict of Worms of 1521. It has been argued that this was a decisive moment in the history of the German Reformation. Henceforth, the princes and the towns of the Empire considered that they possessed a constitutional right of religious reform. Charles was in no position to force a retreat upon the Diet. He urgently required money and troops from Germany for his struggle with the French and the Ottomans. He could only resolve to reinstate the Edict of Worms at a later date.

By 1529 Charles was ready to initiate firmer action against the German Lutherans. He had enjoyed significant successes over the French in Italy and the Ottoman threat in eastern Europe was receding. He therefore instructed Ferdinand to pursue a more aggressive line against the Lutherans at another meeting of the Diet at Speyer in 1529. Ferdinand demanded a repeal of the 1526 Speyer decisions and a return to the 1521 Edict of Worms. Six Lutheran princes, backed by 14 cities, signed a 'protest' against the Habsburg demands, giving birth to the term 'Protestant' for those who rejected the authority of the Church of Rome. This attempt to use the Imperial Diet as a means of settling religious differences had backfired; the two sides were now more divided than ever.

In 1530 Charles was crowned by the Pope as Holy Roman Emperor. The occasion was largely symbolic but he took the opportunity to press upon the Pope the necessity of convoking a General Council of the Church to help heal religious divisions in Germany. The Pope called, instead, for stern measures against the German Protestants. However, Charles, more appreciative of the weakness of his authority in Germany, stuck to a conciliatory course. He summoned the German estates to a Diet at Augsburg in the same year in order to 'settle disputes, to commit previous error to the mercy of our Saviour, to hear, to understand and weigh the opinion of each man with love and charity, and thus come to live again in one Church and state'. Having brought the two sides together, it was now the turn of the Protestant and Catholic leaders to define their positions and to commence negotiations. The Protestant leaders started off on a reasonably moderate note (Luther was still outlawed and therefore absent), but relations between the two sides were soon soured. The Protestants announced that they would never submit to papal supremacy over a reunited Church. The Catholic negotiators proved to be even more unbending and insisted on a rigid adherence to Catholic orthodoxy. The Protestants departed from the Diet, issuing a statement of their beliefs, the Augsburg Confession, which was to become the official credo of a separatist Protestant Church in Germany. The remaining Catholics signalled their implacable hostility to Protestantism in the Augsburg Recess:

> This doctrine (i.e. of the Protestants) which has been already condemned, has given rise to much misleading error among the common people. They have lost all true reverence, all Christian honour, discipline, the fear of God and charity to their neighbour – they are utterly forgotten.

The Diet reaffirmed the Edict of Worms and gave the Protestants six months in which to return to the Catholic Church. Charles had, at first, been disappointed by the rigidity of the Catholic negotiating position. However, he was genuinely scandalised by the heretical theology of the Protestants and appalled to hear that they were attending Lutheran sermons in Augsburg itself. He therefore endorsed the Augsburg Recess and its ultimatum to the Protestants. In secret, he sounded out the possibility of employing force to crush Protestantism in the Empire, but the Catholic princes refused to support such a scheme. The Augsburg Diet was a significant turning-point in the history of the Protestant Reformation in Germany. The Protestants were persuaded that Charles and his Catholic allies would never admit to the errors of the Catholic Church, and they therefore formed themselves into a defensive military alliance, called the League of Schmalkalden. The Empire now contained an organised and armed Protestant opposition. Yet in the 1530s Charles was to continue to seek a religious reconciliation in Germany, despite the failure of such a policy in the 1520s.

* Charles was again absent from Germany between 1532 and 1541. The German Protestants took advantage of his absence and consolidated their position within the Empire. During the 1530s it was, above all, the Protestant princes in Germany who became the real champions of the Reformation. Luther, himself, who at times in the 1520s appeared to be leading a popular national movement for reform, accepted the princes' political protection of the reformed church. The willingness of the princes to defend the Lutheran Church was best expressed through the League of Schmalkalden. It gained military strength and unity of purpose and even treated with foreign powers in order to strengthen the position of Protestantism in Germany. Although it somewhat disingenuously professed loyalty to the Emperor, the princes utilised the league to ensure the survival of reformed churches within their own territories. Meanwhile, Charles was beset with relentless pressures outside Germany. In the 1530s he was seldom free from French and Ottoman intrigue and provocation and the German Protestant princes were not slow to exploit such difficulties. In 1534, for example, the Schmalkaldic League, in collusion with the French, restored the Protestant Duke of Württemberg to his important south German duchy. Charles could do nothing to punish such open defiance, as he was preparing to attack Muslim forces in the Mediterranean. The papacy, too, gave little comfort to Charles. Clement VII resented Habsburg domination in Italy and in 1533, for example, conspired with the French crown against Charles. Throughout the 1530s Charles remained frustrated and embittered at the growth of Protestantism in Germany. However, he rejected as impracticable any military operations against the League of Schmalkalden. He was too preoccupied elsewhere and doubted his military capacity to defeat the League. In practice, therefore, his policy amounted to one of grudging toleration of Protestantism. In 1532, in the Religious Peace of Nurem-

berg, Charles proclaimed peace in the Empire and permitted Protestant territories to maintain reformed churches until such time as a General Council of the Church reviewed the situation. The peace was significant as for the first time Lutheran heresy was legally tolerated within the Empire. In return, Charles obtained German assistance in his campaign against the Ottomans. In 1539 the Ottoman shadow again menaced the Empire from the east and Charles required substantial support from Germany. In the 1539 Interim of Frankfurt he made further concessions to the Protestants, promising that no legal proceedings would be taken against them for a period of six months at least. He explained his actions:

> Our intention is to meet them (the Protestants) on certain individual points which do not affect the fundamentals of our faith, and to avoid stirring up irritation by refusing things, either for a time or for ever.

The Frankfurt settlement was perceived by Charles as being 'interim', or temporary, as he still pinned his hopes on the summoning of a General Council of the Church. However, the fate of his pleas in the 1530s for the calling of a General Council did not give much ground for optimism. Pope Clement VII had proved unco-operative. At first, under pressure from Charles, he vacillated. However, he abandoned any pretence of convoking a council, after some pressure from the French, who could only benefit from the continuation of Habsburg tribulations in the Empire. In 1534 Pope Clement died and was succeeded by Pope Paul III. The new pontiff recognised the urgency of Church reform and was anxious to work towards Christian reunification. When he agreed to a summoning of a General Council in 1537 Charles' persistence appeared to be bearing fruit. However, for a second time the plan for a Council was sabotaged by the French.

* In 1541, disillusioned by the continual postponement of a General Council, Charles planned what was to be his last real attempt to bring the two sides of the religious divide in Germany together. By this time, his own position in Europe and Germany had improved. Tensions with the French had temporarily eased. The Schmalkaldic League was now weakened by internal divisions. Its leader, Philip of Hesse, was publicly discredited when he committed the capital offence of bigamy. Charles, therefore, felt sufficiently confident that he could bring the Protestant and Catholic leaders round to some form of reconciliation. He summoned the Imperial Diet to meet at Regensburg in 1541. He attended in person, hoping that his own participation would advance genuine negotiations. For two months the politicians and theologians debated areas of difference and searched for a consensus. The Protestant leaders at Regensburg showed some willingness to compromise, but Luther and other absent Protestant leaders were not prepared to accept any

sacrifice of principle. However, it was the papal representatives who most dismayed Charles at Regensburg. Their instructions from the Pope hardly suggested a spirit of give and take:

> If they say to you that the settlement of this dispute is urgent, you are to say to them that the salvation of men's souls is yet more urgent.

Throughout the proceedings the papal spokesmen constantly obstructed progress. Yet, after two decades of religious division in Germany, it is arguable that both sides were by now too deeply entrenched in their respective positions for any settlement to be possible. The earnest debate at Regensburg really masked fundamental and, by now, irreconcilable differences. No compromise could be found. The Diet signalled the end of any real hope, on all sides, of arriving at a compromise. It also signalled the end of Charles' real commitment to peaceful negotiation with the German Protestants. At first, he turned away bitterly from his German difficulties and directed his energies against his Muslim opponents. He then began to formulate a much tougher approach to the religious problems of the Empire.

c) The Resort to Force, 1541–55

In the 12 years that followed the failure at Regensburg, Charles remained, for the most part, in Germany and put the religious division in the Empire at the top of his list of priorities. He maintained the appearance, at least, of persisting with peaceful methods. In January 1544 he called a meeting of the Imperial Diet at Speyer and appealed again for reconciliation. However, behind his conciliatory words he was by now planning a military campaign against the League of Schmalkalden. His main purpose at Speyer was probably to win over those Protestant princes whose allegiance to Lutheranism was wavering. At a further meeting of the Diet at Speyer in 1546 the Protestant leaders realised that negotiations were a sham and began to prepare their forces against an imperial attack. Remarkably, perhaps, Charles still clung to the hope that the long-awaited General Council of the Church called by Paul III might still forestall the necessity of military action against the Protestants. The Council at last met in 1545, at the imperial city of Trent in the southern Alps. It was officially in session until 1549. However, during the critical period of its existence, in 1546 and 1547, the proceedings of the Council greatly disappointed Charles. He had hoped to see some of the real institutional defects of the Church tackled by the Council, so that some Protestant criticisms could be met. However, under strict papal control, the Council evaded such issues and proceeded, instead, to restate established Church doctrine in an unhelpfully conservative manner. In 1547 the Council became even more an instrument of the papacy when it was moved from Trent to the papal city of Bologna. Charles was vexed and boycotted the Council. Paul III died in 1549 and was succeeded by Julius III. In 1551 a reconvened Council proved to be equally unhelpful to Charles. It was the last meeting of the General Council in Charles' lifetime.

The whole experience of seeking reconciliation through a General Council of the Church had been a frustrating and dispiriting one for Charles. Some commentators have been very critical of his belief that a Council would arrive at a religious settlement acceptable to both Catholics and Protestants. This is primarily because Charles' hopes for such a Council were not shared by the other interested parties. The papacy was consistently reluctant to convene a Council at all. It had a long history of opposition to the very idea of a General Council, tending to regard the 'conciliar movement' as a conspiracy to supplant papal control of the Church. Moreover, in Charles' time, the Holy See was anxious to guarantee papal supremacy over the Council's proceedings, and opposed convoking a council on their opponents' 'home ground' in Germany. The Protestants, on the other hand, demanded a 'free, Christian Council', meaning a council free from papal control. They saw religious division as a German issue, to be discussed at a Church Council held in Germany. They were also eager to keep their options open and demurred at Charles' proposal that the Council's decisions should be binding on all participants.

* It is not absolutely certain at what point after the 1541 Regensburg Diet Charles determined to impose a military solution upon Germany. However, it is clear that between 1541 and 1544 Charles' inclination towards such a solution hardened into a fixed resolve. Of greater interest than the precise timing of such a decision are the reasons why Charles abandoned a policy of dialogue and opted instead for force.

Firstly, the international context was important. In the early 1540s Charles made significant breakthroughs as an international statesman, concluding an alliance with Henry VIII of England in 1543 and bringing the war with France to an end in the Peace of Crépy in 1544. He was now better able to concentrate his resources against his opponents in Germany. His Spanish armies could be directed to Germany and the German Protestants would be denied French aid. Between 1541 and 1544 Charles' relations with the papacy had been strained; however, by 1546 relations had improved and Charles was able to sign a formal alliance in which the Pope agreed to provide troops and financial assistance to Charles for an assault upon Protestantism in the Empire.

Secondly, developments in Germany helped to persuade Charles that military action against the Protestants was necessary. The Regensburg Diet of 1541 had finally demonstrated that the prospect of a negotiated peace was illusory. The urgency of military action was underlined by the remarkable successes of the Protestants in Germany after Regensburg. By 1545 both the north-east and the north-west of Germany had fallen to Protestant domination, as had large parts of the south-west. It began to look as though the whole of the Empire might fall to the Protestants. At the same time, Charles was beginning to receive indications of support from some prominent, but disaffected, Protestant princes in Germany. The most notable of these was Maurice of Saxony (the ruler of the smaller of the two Saxon states), who saw some political advantage in treating with the emperor.

In the summer of 1546 Charles began his military operations against the League of Schmalkalden. It is always important for historians to distinguish between the public statements given by politicians and statesmen to explain their actions, and their real motives. Charles' public justification for the use of force stressed his political duty as Emperor to restore imperial authority and, with it, peace and good order in his lands. However, some of his private correspondence reveals a more explicitly religious motivation. He wrote to his sister Mary in June 1541:

> 1 Unless we take immediate action all the estates of Germany may
>   lose their faith, and the Netherlands may follow. After fully
>   considering all these points, I decided to begin by levying war on
>   Hesse and Saxony [Philip of Hesse and the elector John Frederick
> 5 of Saxony] as disturbers of the peace, and to open the campaign in
>   the lands of the duke of Brunswick. This pretext will not long
>   conceal the true purpose of this war of religion, but it will serve to
>   divide the Protestants from the beginning. We shall be able to
>   work out the rest as we go along.

Yet it can be argued that both religious and political considerations determined Charles' decision to go to war against Protestantism in Germany. He certainly wanted to end the schism in the Church and to restore obedience to the true, Catholic faith. But, at the same time, he wished to reassert imperial authority and to punish political disloyalty within the Empire. Such dual motivations remind us how often religious and political issues were intermingled in early modern European history.

When Charles began his military campaign against the League of Schmalkalden in 1546 the league's position appeared to be strong. They were numerically a match for Charles' armies and they were well prepared for war. However, they were divided among themselves and their forces were badly led. The league's advances in the early stages of the war were not followed up. By the end of 1546 Charles had established his armies in southern Germany. Troops had arrived from Italy and the Netherlands, and they were soon to be followed by hardened Spanish troops led by the Duke of Alba. Charles' prospects of success were greatly enhanced in October 1546 when Maurice of

Saxony broke with the Protestant princes and brought his armies over to Charles' side. Maurice attacked the elector John Frederick's lands in Saxony. This stunned the league and forced its leaders to send armies north to support the elector. Charles' path northwards was now cleared. By the spring of 1547, Charles' armies had advanced along the river Danube, imposing imperial authority on some rebel cities as they went. Alba had advanced spectacularly down the Rhineland. It now only remained for the imperial armies to join forces and to close in upon the league's armies in Saxony. The Protestant armies were easily beaten at the Battle of Mühlberg in April 1547. The elector, John Frederick of Saxony, was captured and imprisoned and Philip of Hesse surrendered soon afterwards. Charles now had undisputed control over most of the Empire. Having destroyed the League of Schmalkalden, all the gains of German Protestantism appeared to be under threat.

* It is remarkable, therefore, that within five years the situation had been entirely reversed and Charles' triumph had been undone. In 1552 his armies were easily dispersed by Protestant forces and the Emperor was forced to flee Germany across the Alps only narrowly escaping capture. Why, then, was it that his apparent success of 1547 was so short-lived? In international politics, the tide was running against him once again. From 1551 the Ottomans were advancing further into eastern Europe and were diverting Habsburg attentions away from Germany. The French were causing still greater difficulties. After Mühlberg they intrigued with Germany's Protestant princes and came to an alliance with them in the Treaty of Chambord in 1552. Their intervention in the Protestant revolt of the same year was of crucial military importance. As imperial forces contended with Protestant armies inside Germany, the French overran Habsburg territory in the west. Finally, the papacy did a great deal to undermine Charles' position after Mühlberg. Charles felt that his victory over Protestantism in Germany would be greatly reinforced if a General Council of the Church tackled ecclesiastical abuses within Catholic Christendom. However, relations between Charles and the papacy greatly deteriorated in the second half of the 1540s. The papacy viewed Charles' triumph at Mühlberg with intense unease; a victorious Emperor might use his power to impose a Habsburg hegemony upon Europe as a whole, and in so doing gravely threaten the Holy See's own freedom of action. Hence, the papacy remained, as we have seen, unco-operative on moves to reform the Church through a General Council. Furthermore, the papacy again conspired with the King of France in order to find common means of combatting Habsburg successes.

Inside Germany, the hollowness of Charles' victory became even more evident. Charles had defeated the League of Schmalkalden in battle, but the princes and cities of northern Germany were still loyal to the Reformation. And even in those parts of Germany under the Emperor's control, the Protestant faith survived, despite the defeat of its leaders in battle. Charles often gave the impression that he under-estimated the depth of religious feeling behind Protestantism. After Mühlberg he seemed to believe that he could dictate to his German subjects the form of their religious beliefs and practices. This he sought to do at the Diet of Augsburg, which met in 1547 and 1548. The religious settlement, expressed in the Interim of Augsburg, that Charles demanded the Empire accept, was a traditional one which made practically no concessions to the Protestants. Germany's Protestant leaders rejected it as a dictated imposition of unreformed Catholicism. Popular disaffection was reflected in the catchphrase of the period:

> Do not trust the Interim,
> He has the Devil hind of him.

Thus Charles only succeeded in enforcing the Interim in areas under his military control. Opposition to the Augsburg settlement was based on political as well as religious grounds. Even the Catholic princes were reluctant to support Charles because his victory appeared to signal a marked revival of imperial authority at their own expense. Catholic opposition was made even easier by the unhelpful attitude of the papacy. Rome refused to recognise the Interim for over a year, regarding it as an infringement of its own jurisdiction. The situation was worse, of course, for the Protestant princes, who feared a loss of their religious liberty as well as their political power. They began to organise resistance, centred on the northern territories that had eluded Charles' control. By 1550 they had approached Henry II, who had become the new French king in 1547, to elicit his support for a counter-offensive against Charles. Early in 1551 Maurice of Saxony, who had been so instrumental in securing Charles' victory, deserted him and returned his allegiance to the Protestant cause. Maurice felt that he had not been adequately rewarded by Charles and, sensing the way the wind was blowing in Germany, decided he had most to gain from supporting a Protestant revolt against Charles. By 1552 the stage was set for Charles' nemesis in Germany. He was acutely short of money and had been unable to keep his imperial armies in Germany. He had been blind to the mounting evidence of internal and external conspiracy against him and had made no plans to counter a serious rebellion. Hence the revolt of 1552, launched by northern Protestants and Maurice of Saxony in conjunction with the French, met little imperial resistance. Charles' ignominious flight from Germany marked the end of his ambition to impose his will upon the Empire, in both political and religious matters.

Charles' flight also marked the end of his direct involvement in the religious affairs of the Empire. He authorised Ferdinand to initiate negotiations in Germany. Ferdinand was empowered to make whatever concessions to the Protestants were necessary to restore peace and order in the Empire. Charles, for his part, recognised that major concessions were now inevitable, but he balked at giving his personal approval to them. When the Imperial Diet met at Augsburg in February 1555 to work out a new religious settlement Charles refused to attend;

> My reason is only this question of religion, in regard to which I have an unconquerable scruple.

The Diet of Augsburg brought to an end decades of religious division in Germany. It was agreed that the ruler of a territory should determine its religion. Those who could not accept their prince's faith could emigrate to other territories. The imperial cities were to tolerate both Catholic and Protestant confessions. The Diet of Augsburg was a turning-point in the history of the Empire. It was at last admitted that the unity of the Church had been permanently lost. The princes were undoubtedly the victors in the long struggle between imperial authority and princely independence.

d) Assessment

Charles clearly failed in his aim to maintain a unified Church in Germany. However, it is arguable that his position was an impossible one and that any Holy Roman Emperor would have been as impotent as Charles in preventing a schism in the Church. Charles was, of course, greatly handicapped by his other imperial obligations and distractions. The French and the Turks, in particular, made it extremely difficult for him to concentrate his attention on the Empire. In addition, the papacy gave him little support and thwarted his attempts to reunify the Church through the mediation of a General Council. However, above all, it can be argued, the Holy Roman Emperor lacked the power to dictate to the princes and the cities of the Empire. He could only rule effectively in co-operation with them, and their support in suppressing Lutheranism in Germany was clearly not forthcoming. Both Protestant and Catholic princes were determined to resist the sort of imposition of imperial authority that would have been necessary to force Catholicism upon the Empire as a whole. In this context, it is instructive to compare Charles' successful suppression of Protestantism in Spain and the Netherlands (see pages 31–2 and pages 19–20) with his failure to do so in Germany. In Spain and the Netherlands he enjoyed both the political power and the support of his leading subjects, which enabled him to check the spread of Protestant ideas. In Germany he was forced into a long period of appeasing Protestantism because he lacked the power to suppress it. When he tried to impose Catholicism in the late 1540s, the limits of his power and support were quickly exposed after his short-lived victory at Mühlberg.

Nevertheless, criticisms of Charles' responses to the Reformation in

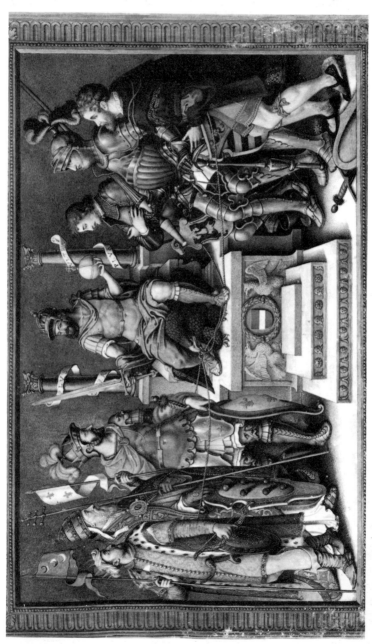

A symbolic presentation of the Emperor's victories

Germany have been made. Charles, it can be argued, failed to accord the problem a sufficiently high priority in the 1520s and 1530s. Therefore, by the 1540s it was too late to reverse the gains of the Protestants. In addition, Charles can be accused of failing to provide a clear and consistent lead to his German subjects. On the one hand, he alienated some Protestant sympathisers with the belligerence of his condemnations of Lutheranism. On the other, for most of his reign he pursued a policy of conciliation and appeasement. It can also be claimed that he failed to understand the real nature of the religious division in Germany. He did not appreciate the position of the conservative hierarchy of the Catholic Church whose members believed that if an inch was surrendered to the Protestants they would take a mile. He also failed to understand how deeply-felt were the beliefs of the Protestants. They were not likely to trade their principles for the sake of a fudged compromise with the Catholic Church. And Charles failed, finally, in the 1540s, to realise that he lacked the political and military resources to impose more than a temporary settlement upon the Empire by force of arms.

2 The Muslim Challenge

a) The Mediterranean

Charles' major theatre of conflict with Muslim power was the Mediterranean. Since the late fifteenth century the Ottomans had built up a large and well-equipped fleet. It was based in the eastern Mediterranean and posed a particular threat to isolated Christian communities there, such as the island of Rhodes (see map, page 100). It was also a potential threat to both Habsburg lands and shipping throughout the Mediterranean. However, the greatest danger to the Habsburgs came from Muslim pirates (corsairs) based closer to home, on the Barbary coast of north Africa. They came from fiercely anti-Spanish communities, many of whom had been driven from Spain to Africa during the Christian reconquest of Spain. The port of Algiers was their naval base and headquarters. Their strength was formidable. The corsair fleet was large and mobile, and it was daringly led by the pirate admiral Kheireddin Barbarossa (Redbeard). The corsair threat to the empire of Charles V was manifold. Firstly, from their north African bases corsair galleys were in an ideal position to attack Habsburg shipping in the Mediterranean. This imperilled the lines of communication and supply connecting Spain to its Mediterranean empire. Grain supplies to Spain from Sicily were particularly vulnerable. Secondly, the corsair fleet pillaged the coastlines of the Habsburgs' Mediterranean lands – the Balearic islands, Italy and Spain itself. From them they seized treasures, grain and slaves for their galleys. Thirdly, as King of

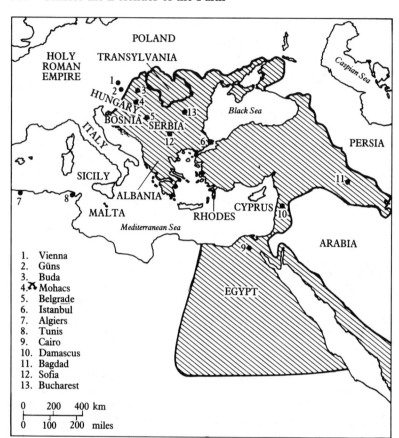

POLAND

HOLY
ROMAN   TRANSYLVANIA
EMPIRE
          1.
          2.
HUNGARY   3.
          4.
BOSNIA   5.   13.   Black Sea
          SERBIA
          12.   6.

Caspian Sea

PERSIA

ITALY

SICILY

ALBANIA   11.

7   8.
       MALTA   CYPRUS
                   RHODES   10.
       Mediterranean Sea

ARABIA

9.

EGYPT

1. Vienna
2. Güns
3. Buda
4. Mohacs
5. Belgrade
6. Istanbul
7. Algiers
8. Tunis
9. Cairo
10. Damascus
11. Bagdad
12. Sofia
13. Bucharest

0   200   400 km
0   100   200 miles

The Ottoman Empire under Suleiman II

Spain, Charles inherited important, but isolated, naval bases on the
north African coast, such as Oran, Bougie and Tripoli. The Spanish
fleet depended on access to them in order to police Spain's Mediterranean sea-lanes. But they too were vulnerable to corsair attack. Lastly,
in 1518 Barbarossa's corsair fleet was placed under the protection of the
Ottoman Sultan. This combination of the Ottoman and corsair fleets
greatly strengthened Muslim naval power in the Mediterranean.

As we have seen (page 85) Charles V was strongly attracted to the
idea of a 'Holy War' against Islam. As King of Spain he had an
additional incentive to combat Muslim power in the Mediterranean.
His Spanish subjects, steeped in the traditions of the *Reconquista* (see
page 85), were deeply intolerant of Islam and were eager to extend the
victories of the *Reconquista* to the Muslim strongholds in north Africa.
In addition, the mainland of Spain contained a large north African
population (the Moors) who had been forcibly converted from Islam to

Christianity in the early sixteenth century. These *Moriscos* had not been successfully assimilated into Spanish society and there were justifiable fears that their sympathies lay more with the Muslims of north Africa than with Spain. Thus Spanish feelings of insecurity about the Muslim menace in the Mediterranean were intensified by fears of a fifth column in Spain ready to ally itself with Infidel invaders.

In the 1520s Charles failed to check Muslim influence in the Mediterranean. In 1522 the Ottomans achieved a notable success when they captured the island of Rhodes from the Christian knights of St. John. The capture of Rhodes gave the Ottoman fleets supremacy in the eastern Mediterranean and provided a base from which to mount attacks on Italy and on Spain itself. The seizure of Rhodes was an early achievement of Suleiman II ('the Magnificent') the sultan of the Ottoman Empire from 1520. In 1529 Barbarossa achieved a similar success in the western Mediterranean, when he expelled a Spanish garrison from the Peñon, a fortified rock at the harbour entrance to Algiers. In the same year a Spanish fleet of eight galleys was destroyed off Ibiza, an island close to the Spanish mainland.

* In the early 1530s Charles was able to devote more attention to challenging Muslim seapower in the Mediterranean. He was greatly helped in this task by the able Genoese admiral, Andrea Doria, who had abandoned his French ally in 1528 and transferred his fleet to Charles' command. In the following year, the Peace of Cambrai started a seven year respite for Charles from war against the French. In 1532 he was able to enjoy his first success against Muslim seapower when Doria seized the ports of Coron and Patras in Greece. Charles had demonstrated an ability to strike back into the eastern Mediterranean. However, the struggle for the control of the Mediterranean did not go all his own way. Suleiman responded by appointing Barbarossa admiral of the Ottoman fleet. Barbarossa now had under his command the pirate ships of north Africa and the smaller Ottoman navy. He first deployed his strengthened naval capacity in a series of raids on Habsburg Italy. Next, in 1534, he mounted an assault on the north African city of Tunis; it fell, and a Muslim ruler allied to Charles V was ousted. The capture of Tunis was followed by Muslim raids on the Balearic islands and on the Valencian coast of Spain.

It was the loss of Tunis that stung Charles into more concerted action against Barbarossa. Tunis commanded the narrow sea between Africa and Sicily and its loss exposed Sicily and Habsburg shipping to great danger. Strategic considerations were reinforced by religious ones. Charles resolved to recapture Tunis to mark the beginnings of a Holy War against the Infidel in north Africa. When he finally set sail from Barcelona with his fleet, he did so beneath a banner of the crucified Christ. Yet it is impossible to ignore the emphatically personal terms in which he saw the Tunisian campaign. He clearly felt that his knightly honour and reputation had been sorely injured by Barbarossa, and he was anxious for revenge. Hence, the determination to lead his forces in person. The attempts of Cardinal Tavera to dissuade him from doing so were in vain:

> Look how much depends on your person, and how you would leave your kingdoms if, for our sins, some disaster should befall you. God forbid! And if this should not move you, remember that Your Majesty's son is still a child.

Adamant about pursuing a triumphant victory at Tunis, Charles ignored his present difficulties in Germany, and his brother Ferdinand's in Hungary. The *Cortes* of Castile was, as usual, prevailed upon to contribute generously; the papacy, typically, gave modestly. A vast fleet of about 400 ships and 60,000 men was assembled at Sardinia and crossed over to Tunis in May 1535. Charles led his troops successfully against the fortress of La Goletta. Meanwhile, the Christian captives in Tunis took the opportunity to rebel. Finally, the Habsburg army stormed the city and slaughtered its inhabitants. Charles later commented:

> Because the town's inhabitants did not appear to greet their restored sovereign as they should have done, and as he had a right to expect, we allowed the pillage of the place as punishment for their obstinacy.

The greater part of Barbarossa's fleet (over 80 galleys) was captured and Barbarossa himself was forced to flee to Algiers.

The capture of Tunis was Charles' only decisive victory against the Muslim powers of the Mediterranean. It was, in particular, a great personal triumph. To much of Europe he was now a great soldier-prince, and a champion of Christendom against the Infidel. In strategic terms, Charles' triumph appeared considerable. Tunis was a useful base from which to pursue corsair ships sailing from harbours in north Africa. More importantly, he was now better able to intercept Muslim shipping plying between Algiers and the Ottoman Empire in the east. However, in retrospect, the victory was not as great as it appeared at the time. Tunis was entrusted again to a Muslim ally, who ruled the city as a vassal of Charles, but whose reliability was uncertain. Secondly, it is clear now that it was really only the capture of Algiers that would have ensured Charles respite from the corsair menace. After Tunis Charles realised that he had neither the resources for an attack on Algiers, nor the time to spare from other pressing imperial commitments. Thus Barbarossa continued to harry Habsburg territories and shipping in the Mediterranean with his customary persistence and success.

  * The continuing vulnerability of Charles' position in the Mediterranean was further, and dramatically, underlined in 1536 when the

French king, Francis I, concluded a formal alliance with the Ottomans. Charles' main European antagonist was now in league with his greatest rival outside of Europe. Europe was shocked by such an unholy alliance between the cross of Christianity and the crescent of Islam. Charles denounced the French king as a traitor to Christendom. Francis tried to justify his alliance with the Ottomans by pointing out that his treaty with them guaranteed Christian interests within the Ottoman Empire providing, for example, for the protection of pilgrims and holy places. Nevertheless, it is obvious that the alliance was forged, above all, on the basis of mutual hostility to the Habsburgs. The treaty inflicted much damage on Charles' Mediterranean interests in the years to come. The French exploited the alliance to pressurise Charles' position in Italy. In 1537, for example, the Ottoman navy attacked Naples to coincide with a French land offensive. The French and the Ottomans also co-ordinated their attacks on the Habsburgs' maritime communications in the Mediterranean. Furthermore, in the 1530s and 1540s Barbarossa was given valuable havens for his ships in Marseilles and Toulon.

It suited Habsburg propaganda to portray the King of France as an international Judas Iscariot, betraying Christendom for his own ends. Charles' outrage was in some ways justified. He genuinely saw himself as a defender of Christendom and as a crusader against the evils of Islam. To ally with a Muslim against any Christian would have been abhorrent to him. Yet the historian who described his policies towards Islam as 'the admixture of idealism with practical politics' is surely correct. When the opportunity arose for a Holy War against Islam he was easily fired with crusading zeal. At other times he was more pragmatic. When the need arose he accepted the necessity of making deals with Islam in the interests of his wider imperial security. He was periodically in diplomatic contact with the Muslim Shah of Persia, encouraging him to harass his Ottoman neighbours. He was prepared, as we have seen, to co-exist with Muslim rulers in north Africa, as long as they were loyal to him and not to Barbarossa. And in 1547 he negotiated a five year truce with Suleiman himself so that he might consolidate his recent victories in Germany.

In the years immediately following his victory at Tunis in 1535, Charles became convinced of his ability to achieve further such triumphs in the Mediterranean. In 1538 the Treaty of Nice allowed him a breathing space from the Habsburg–Valois wars. The treaty also temporarily detached the French from their Ottoman allies. This time Charles decided to attack the Ottomans on their home ground. At first he toyed with the idea of an asault on Istanbul, the capital of the Ottoman Empire. However, good sense prevailed, and he chose instead to seek out the Ottoman fleet in its home waters. In preparing for such an enterprise he succeeded in bringing in the active support of both Venice and the papacy. His plans aroused considerable controversy. His Castilian advisers could see little advantage in eastern Mediterranean operations and recommended an assault on Algiers instead. His sister Mary, regent of the Netherlands, protested vehemently, arguing that his European dominions were more needy of attention and perceptively pointing out that a permanent victory over the Ottomans in the eastern Mediterranean was an impossibility given the difficulty of following up initial successes over a period of years. She ended her plea to Charles thus:

1 And in what straits should we be if you were defeated, or never came home again? In the name of God, I implore you, bethink of your duty to God himself. So great a prince as you must only conquer. Defeat is the ultimate crime. Wait but for a year or two.
5 Set your lands in order against a long absence. . . . This is the advice, which in all humility, I offer to you.

Charles was persuaded not to accompany his fleet in person, but he shared none of Mary's pessimism. The showdown came in September 1538 when the Emperor's fleet met a relatively small Ottoman force, commanded by Barbarossa, at Prevesa, off the Albanian coast. Charles' admiral, Doria, was suspicious of the Venetian commanders and, fatefully, held back many of his ships. The under-strength Christian fleet was forced to retreat ignominiously. The consequences of this defeat were more significant than such a half-hearted engagement might suggest. Barbarossa's reputation was greatly enhanced, whilst the odium of defeat attached itself very much to the absent Charles. Venice abandoned the Christian alliance and, in 1540, made a separate peace with the Ottoman Sultan. For the remainder of Charles' life Ottoman domination of the eastern Mediterranean was a fact of life. Charles was forced to think of targets nearer to home.

* By 1541 Charles' thoughts again returned to the prospect of avenging his humiliations at the hands of Barbarossa. This time Algiers was the obvious target. His Spanish realms were likely to be enthusiastic about an expedition to clear Muslim pirates out of neighbouring waters. Indeed, Charles' late wife, Empress Isabella, had frequently urged an attack on Algiers. The city was not well garrisoned and appeared to provide Charles with the opportunity to repeat his earlier victory at Tunis. Above all, Algiers was the root of the problem of Habsburg security in the Mediterranean, as it was from here that Barbarossa masterminded the combined operations of the corsair, Ottoman and French fleets. Charles planned a massive expedition for October 1541. Those who, like Admiral Doria, counselled that this was too late in the season to offer safe weather for such an attack, were soon to be vindicated. Charles personally took charge of a fleet almost as large as that which had vanquished Barbarossa at Tunis. But disaster struck as his troops prepared the assault on Algiers. Charles recalled the events in his memoirs:

1 After a few skirmishes, with everyone already suitably positioned
  to besiege the town and everything ready to batter it down,
  unexpectedly there was a great storm at sea, many vessels were
  lost and even those which lay at anchor were damaged. Every-
5 thing was done to rally our strength to fight the fury of the sea as
  much as against the attacks and assaults of the enemies on land.

Charles pressed on and attempted to attack Algiers with a hopelessly
inadequate force and with equally inadequate supplies. A French agent
reported that Charles lost his clothes and had to survive on a diet of
cats, dogs and grass. His forces were easily driven back and the
survivors re-embarked and set sail for Spain in disarray. About 150
ships and 17,000 men were lost. Charles' reputation as the victor of
Tunis was buried by the humiliation of Algiers. It was his last, real
attempt to discomfit the Muslim powers of the Mediterranean. For the
remainder of his reign the corsair pirates continued to harry his lands
and shipping from their secure base at Algiers.

Charles abandoned any hope of inflicting a conclusive defeat upon
Muslim seapower after the Algiers debacle. The initiative passed to his
enemies and in 1541 a renewed Franco-Ottoman alliance led to joint
naval operations against Charles' shipping. In 1543 the port of Nice was
captured from Charles' ally, the Duke of Savoy, by a combined French
and Ottoman fleet. In 1546 Barbarossa died; he was over 80-years-old.
His mantle was taken over by the equally intrepid Dragut, who
continued successful raids on the Spanish coastline, the Balearic islands
and Sicily. Charles hoped that a truce concluded with Suleiman in 1547
would ease the pressure on him in the Mediterranean. The Sultan
recognised Charles' strengthened position following his victory over the
German Protestants at Mühlberg. Suleiman was also anxious to devote
more resources to his war with Persia. However, Dragut's aggressive
activities continued throughout the truce, despite Charles' protests to
the Sultan. When the truce came to an end in 1551 the Muslim alliance
between Algiers and Istanbul resumed, and in that year the Sultan's
navy, commanded by Dragut, captured Tripoli in north Africa from
the knights of St. John. This gave Charles' enemies an important base
in the central basin of the Mediterranean. In 1552 a Spanish fleet,
commanded by the aged Doria, was defeated off the coast of Italy. In
Charles' remaining years, Muslim forces made further in-roads into
Habsburg territory. In 1554 they captured Peñon de Vélez, and in 1555
Bougie, leaving only four surviving Spanish outposts in north Africa.

Charles clearly failed to realise his ambition of defeating Muslim
power in the Mediterranean. Yet he faced formidable difficulties. His
other imperial obligations only afforded him short periods in which to
concentrate his resources on this task. Furthermore, he was left very
much on his own in defending Christendom from Muslim aggression
against southern Europe. While the French actually supported the

Sultan, other Christian powers tended to look the other way. Venice, for example, with its large and experienced fleet, was more interested in furthering its own commercial and territorial ambitions than in supporting the Emperor against the Sultan. Charles' task was a daunting one in other ways too. Guaranteeing the protection of the Habsburgs' extensive territories and sea-lanes in the Mediterranean was, in many ways, an impossibility as Charles lacked the naval and financial resources to enable him to do so. Nevertheless, he can be credited with some achievements. He did secure southern Europe from all but coastal raids, Malta remained an important Christian garrison, and, although Charles was unable to check pirate raids in the western Mediterranean, they never attained complete ascendancy there. Such considerations have led some historians to conclude that Charles was successful in holding the line against Muslim naval mastery in the Mediterranean. It has further been argued that he thereby laid the foundations for his son,

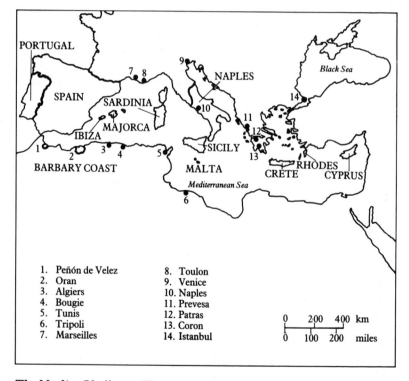

1. Peñón de Velez	8. Toulon
2. Oran	9. Venice
3. Algiers	10. Naples
4. Bougie	11. Prevesa
5. Tunis	12. Patras
6. Tripoli	13. Coron
7. Marseilles	14. Istanbul

The Muslim Challenge: The Mediterranean

Philip's more decisive defeat of Muslim sea-power at the battle of Lepanto in 1571.

Yet, if Charles' performance is measured against his own professed objectives, his failure becomes more apparent. He favoured a forward policy in the Mediterranean, aiming to revive Europe's crusading spirit and crush Muslim naval strongholds in the eastern Mediterranean and north Africa. Prevesa (1538) and Algiers (1541) ended these hopes. Even in defensive terms, Charles' record is not very convincing. The coastlines of Naples and Sicily were never secured from Muslim attack, whilst Barbarossa and Dragut continued to threaten Spain's own doorstep. The impact of all this on Charles' international reputation was very damaging. Europe's most powerful monarch was bearded time and again by Muslim pirates and by the ships of an Infidel Emperor. In this context, it can be argued that Philip II's later successes in the Mediterranean owed less to the work of his father, and more to his own endeavours.

b) Eastern Europe

The Muslim threat existed not only on the seas of the Mediterranean, but also in the east of Europe, from the mainland Ottoman Empire. Here, in the Balkans (see map, page 100), lay the unstable and dangerous boundary between the Ottoman Empire and Christendom. In the fifteenth century Ottoman armies had advanced into the Balkans and overrun Serbia, Bosnia and Albania. The Ottoman armies had earned for themselves an awesome reputation. Hungary provided the final obstacle to their advance into Christian Europe, and it now acted as a buffer zone between Islam and Christianity. The fall of Hungary would expose Austria and the heartlands of Europe to Ottoman attack. This danger gave rise to what has been termed the 'Great Fear' in early modern history – the widespread panic that Christendom would be overrun by barbarian Muslim hordes. The Christian perception of Muslims was, of course, ill-founded, but the terrors it produced were historically significant in their own right. Charles, as Holy Roman Emperor, and his brother Ferdinand, Archduke of Austria from 1522, were naturally very conscious of the Ottoman threat to the Habsburg lands in central Europe and to Germany. In addition Christian Europe looked upon the Holy Roman Emperor as the defender of the security of Christendom.

The aggressive designs of Suleiman II in Europe appeared to be confirmed in 1521 when his armies attacked and captured Belgrade. The city provided a gateway to Hungary. In 1526 Suleiman decided that the moment was opportune to advance into Hungary. The Hungarian nobles were squabbling amongst themselves and his own army was growing frustrated at the failure to follow up the Belgrade success. A huge Ottoman army of 100,000 men met King Louis of

Hungary's forces at Mohacs, north-west of Belgrade. Louis's army was routed and Louis himself was killed a few days later. The Ottoman armies advanced further and seized the Hungarian capital of Buda. Although Suleiman soon withdrew his troops from the capital, he retained control of the whole of Hungary south of Buda. King Louis had died without leaving a direct male heir, and Charles' brother, Ferdinand, as the late king's brother-in-law, was elected his successor. However, Ferdinand succeeded, in practice, only to those parts of the kingdom unoccupied by the Ottomans. Furthermore, he had to wage war against a rival to the throne, John Zapolya, the powerful Duke of Transylvania. Zapolya was defeated in 1527, and fled to Transylvania, where he proclaimed his independence.

Charles was displeased by these developments. He saw that the involvement of the Habsburgs in Hungary would enmesh the dynasty in unpredictable conflicts with the neighbouring Ottomans. He also realised that Zapolya would provide a useful anti-Habsburg ally for them. Other problems demanded his attention, and he was prepared to sacrifice Hungary, despite the risk of exposing central Europe to Ottoman attack. He also appreciated that the Castilian *Cortes* would refuse to finance Habsburg adventures in Eastern Europe.

* In 1529 Suleiman launched another offensive on Europe, but this time the target was Vienna, the capital of Habsburg Austria. His armies re-captured the city of Buda and overran the rest of Hungary. Charles, meanwhile, was preoccupied with problems in the Empire, and afforded little asistance to Ferdinand. In September the Ottoman army reached Vienna and laid siege to the city. However, the Ottomans faced stout resistance and they were hampered by disease and atrocious weather. Their lines of communication and supply were by now severely over-extended. Suleiman abandoned his three week siege and ordered a retreat. Nevertheless, the psychological impact of his offensive was considerable. News of massed Ottoman armies encamped outside the Habsburg capital was received throughout Christendom with alarm. Although the Ottomans had retreated on this occasion there was little to prevent them from returning. Nevertheless, Charles, in a letter to Ferdinand in January 1530, counselled caution in relations with the Sultan. He pointed out that the Habsburg dynasty lacked the resources to take on the Ottomans on its own at this juncture.

Early in 1532 it was becoming clear that Suleiman was planning another offensive against Austria. Charles now had reason to be more optimistic about a religious settlement in Germany. He could, therefore, more realistically contemplate a counter-attack. Such a prospect aroused his crusading instincts, which he revealed in a letter to Empress Isabella in April 1532:

1 I am determined that if the Turk [the Sultan] comes in person, he
   will not do so unless he is at the head of a large army. Therefore I

shall face him myself, and resist his attack with all the forces I can
muster. With God's help – as I act in His cause – I will be helped
5 and favoured, so that He may be served and our Holy Faith be
exalted and strengthened.

First of all, Charles needed to secure the support of his German
subjects. Significant concessions were made to the German Protestants
in the Religious Peace of Nuremberg (June 1532). Charles began to
assemble a large army from Germany and from the rest of his empire.
The Sultan's armies struck in August 1532 with a force reckoned to be
more than 250,000 strong. However, the advance of the Ottomans was
checked, to the surprise of all, at the small forest fortress of Güns, 60
miles south of Vienna. Suleiman opted to retreat. His lines of supply
were stretched and conflict with Persia was escalating on his eastern
front. The summer campaigning season was drawing to a close and
Charles was approaching with reinforcements of some 80,000 men.
Charles entered Vienna on 23 September, sorely disappointed at having
missed the opportunity to lead his armies against the Sultan. However,
he entered the capital as a liberator, crowned in laurels. The aftermath
of his campaign hardly justified such triumphalism. He had to depart
for Italy and leave Ferdinand in command. Ferdinand's German troops
refused to cross into Hungary in pursuit of the Sultan, and they had no
desire to help him in this struggle with Zapolya for the control of
Hungary. In the following year, Ferdinand, now without the active
support of his brother, agreed to a truce with Suleiman. He came out of
it badly, receiving only a small north-western remnant of the kingdom
of Hungary. Yet Charles was probably reasonably satisfied. At least the
situation in the east had been stabilised, and he felt that his intervention
had demonstrated to the Sultan his determination to protect his family
lands in Austria.

   * Conflict between the Habsburgs and the Ottoman Empire flared up
again in the early 1540s. Ferdinand took advantage of the death of
Zapolya in 1540 to seize Buda from the Ottomans and to claim
Zapolya's lands in Transylvania. However the weakness of Ferdinand's
position in Hungary was exposed again when the Sultan drove him out
of Buda in 1541 and installed Zapolya's son, John Sigismund, as a
puppet ruler in Transylvania. Charles was not willing to provide
Ferdinand with direct assistance. He was at this time planning a
campaign against Barbarossa in Algiers. The best he could do was to
adopt a conciliatory approach to the German Protestants at Regensburg, and so encourage them to support Ferdinand. However Ferdinand was fighting a losing battle. In 1543 the Sultan advanced into
Hungary again and extended and consolidated his control over most of
the country. In 1547 Ferdinand reluctantly recognised the inevitability
of Ottoman ascendancy in Hungary. A truce with Suleiman was signed.
Ferdinand kept his corner of Hungary, but only under the protection of

the Sultan, to whom he must pay tribute money. Hungary was for the remainder of Charles V's life a satellite of the Ottoman Empire, and a potential spring-board for offensives against Habsburg Austria.

On the whole, then, Charles delegated the defence of eastern Europe to Ferdinand. The exception was in 1532, when his intervention played some part in persuading Suleiman to abandon his attack on Vienna. Charles had other priorities, and he attached more importance to tackling Muslim power in the Mediterranean than to supporting Ferdinand's defence of Austria and Hungary. According to one of his biographers Charles was the sword against the Infidel in the Mediterranean, and Ferdinand the shield in central Europe. The loss of Hungary exposed central Europe to the danger of Ottoman attack. And the periodic emergencies the Habsburgs consequently faced made it very difficult for them to apply their resources consistently in dealing with their other adversaries, the French and the German Protestants. Yet Charles' limited policy of containment is defensible. In many ways the Ottoman threat to Europe from the east was more apparent than real. The Ottoman armies were, after all, operating a long way from home and so their lines of communication and supply were overstretched. The short summer campaigning season made it difficult for them to consolidate their victories. In addition, Suleiman was faced with distractions of his own. He was pursuing expansionist policies in Egypt and Syria and his conflict with Persia was a periodic diversion. Therefore the risk of the Ottomans overrunning central Europe was slight. As Charles' own resources were severely overstretched, perhaps some kind of stalemate was inevitable.

The Protestant Challenge in Germany: a Chronology

1517   Luther attacks Indulgences and triggers the movement for reform

1519   Charles elected Holy Roman Emperor

1521   Diet of Worms: Luther condemned despite his speech to the Diet

1526   Diet of Speyer: the princes and cities assert the right of religious reform

1529   Diet of Speyer: 'Protest' against Habsburg demands for Catholic uniformity

1530   Diet of Augsburg: Charles fails to reconcile Catholics and Protestants

1531   Formation of League of Schmalkalden: an armed opposition within the Empire

1532   Religious Peace of Nuremberg: Charles declares toleration of Protestantism until a meeting of a General Council

1534	Election of Pope Paul III
1539	Interim of Frankfurt: Charles makes further concessions to the Protestants
1541	Diet of Regensburg: Charles fails to reconcile Protestants and Catholics
1544	Diet of Speyer: Charles appeals for reconciliation but prepares for war
1545	The Council of Trent assembles: Charles hopeful of a religious compromise
1546	Habsburg-Papal alliance: papacy agreed to provide troops and money to defeat Protestantism in Germany
	Diet of Speyer: Charles continues plans for war despite negotiations at Diet
	Charles commences military campaign against German Protestants
1547	Charles boycotts Council of Trent when it is moved to Bologna
	Battle of Mühlberg: Protestants defeated
1547/8	Diet and Interim of Augsburg: Charles attempts to impose Catholic orthodoxy in Germany
1551	Maurice of Saxony deserts Charles and rejoins Protestants
1552	Treaty of Chambord: German Protestants and French plan war against Habsburgs
	Charles defeated and flees Germany
1555	Diet of Augsburg: final defeat of Charles' aim of religious unity in Germany

The Muslim Challenge: a Chronology

	The Mediterranean	*Eastern Europe*
1520	(Accession of Suleiman II)	
1521		Ottomans capture Belgrade
1522	Ottomans capture Rhodes and gain supremacy in eastern Mediterranean	
1526		Ottoman victory at Mohacs over Hungarian forces: king killed and Ferdinand elected successor
1528	Admiral Doria defects to Habsburgs, strengthening Habsburg sea-power	
1529	Barbarossa captures Peñon, at the entrance to Algiers	Ottomans besiege Vienna, capital of Habsburg Austria. But Ottomans retreat

	The Mediterranean	Eastern Europe
1532	Doria captures Coron and Patras in Greece	Ottoman offensive. Retreat after defeat at Güns. Charles arrives with army in Vienna
1533		Ferdinand concludes truce with Ottomans, obtaining small remnant of Hungary
1534	Barbarossa captures Tunis	
1535	Charles recaptures Tunis, in his only decisive victory against Ottomans Franco-Ottoman alliance, aiding Ottoman sea-power	
1538	Ottoman victory at Prevesa Humiliating defeat for Charles' fleet	
1540		Ferdinand captures Buda from Ottomans
1541	Charles' humiliating defeat at Algiers	Ferdinand expelled from Buda
1543		Ottomans offensive in Hungary. They consolidate control over most of Hungary
1546	Death of Barbarossa	
1547		Ferdinand accepts humiliating truce with Ottomans
1551	Dragut captures Tripoli	

Making notes on 'Charles the Defender of the Faith'

1 The Protestant Challenge in Germany

This is an important topic, popular with examiners. Therefore, your notes should be quite detailed. It is important to be familiar with the chronology of Charles' responses to the German Reformation; examiners sometimes set questions which require you to analyse a particular period of Charles' reign in the context of this topic. However, of greater importance are the reasons why Charles failed to prevent the spread of Lutheranism in Germany. Pay particular attention to evidence which helps you to explain this failure. The following headings and questions should provide a suitable framework for your notes.

1.1.   Introduction: Why was Charles so committed to defending Catholicism against internal opposition and the external threat of Islam?
1.2.   Martin Luther, 1517–21
1.2.1. What was the significance of Luther's attack on Indulgences?
1.2.2. Why did Luther's teachings elicit such immediate support in Germany?
1.2.3. Why, and with what results, did Charles invite Luther to Worms?
1.3.   The Years of Appeasement, 1521–41
1.3.1. Interpretations of Charles' policy, 1521–41.
1.3.2. Why did Lutheranism continue to grow in the 1520s?
1.3.3. Assess Charles' responses to Lutheranism, 1521–26.
1.3.4. Assess Charles' progress at the Diet of Speyer, 1529.
1.3.5. Assess Charles' progress at the Diet of Augsburg, 1530.
1.3.6. Assess Charles' progress throughout the 1530s.
1.3.7. Assess Charles' progress at the Diet of Regensburg, 1541.
1.4.   The Resort to Force, 1541–55
1.4.1. Assess Charles' objectives at the Diets of Speyer, 1544 and 1546.
1.4.2. Assess Charles' failure to achieve reconciliation through a meeting of a General Council of the Church.
1.4.3. Why did Charles opt for force in the 1540s?
1.4.4. Account for Charles' military success against the League of Schmalkalden.
1.4.5. Why did Charles' victory prove to be so short-lived, 1547–52?
1.4.6. What was the significance of the Diet of Augsburg in 1555?
1.5.   Assessment: Why was success in suppressing Lutheranism so difficult to achieve? What criticisms can be made of the Emperor himself?

2 The Muslim Challenge

When you are making notes on this topic it is important to become familiar with the chronological 'shape' of the topic. However, it is more important to think about the following historical questions as you proceed:

a) What was the nature of the Muslim threat, and what difficulties did Charles face in dealing with it?
b) How successful was Charles?
c) To what extent did Charles act according to his 'crusading' instincts?

2.1.   The Mediterranean
2.1.1. Why was Muslim power in the Mediterranean a threat to Charles?
2.1.2. Why were the Spanish particularly anti-Muslim?

2.1.3. Assess Muslim successes in the 1520s.
2.1.4. Assess Charles' successes 1532–5.
2.1.5. The Tunis campaign, 1535. Why did it take place? What were the consequences?
2.1.6. The Franco-Ottoman alliance and its consequences.
2.1.7. Charles' attitude to the Franco-Ottoman alliance and his own relations with Muslim powers.
2.1.8. The Prevesa campaign, 1538. Why? What were the consequences?
2.1.9. The Algiers campaign, 1541. Why? What were the consequences?
2.1.10. Conclusions: What were the difficulties of combating Muslim power in the Mediterranean? The historical argument for and against Charles' record.
2.2.   Eastern Europe
2.2.1. Why was Muslim power in eastern Europe so feared?
2.2.2. Ottoman successes in the 1520s.
2.2.3. The Ottoman campaign against Vienna in 1529. Charles' response.
2.2.4. Charles' campaign in 1532. Why and what were the consequences?
2.2.5. Ottoman successes in the 1540s.
2.2.6. Conclusions: How important was Charles' role in eastern Europe? How successful was he? How serious was the Ottoman threat?

Answering essay questions on 'Charles the Defender of the Faith'

1 The Protestant Challenge in Germany
Bear in mind that your understanding of this topic will be enhanced by wider reading (see, for example, *Luther and the German Reformation, 1517–55*, by Keith Randell, in this series).

The most common focus of questions on this topic is on the reasons why Charles failed to check the growth of Lutheranism in Germany. Such questions are likely to be of two types. Firstly, examiners sometimes ask straightforward 'Why' questions. For example:

1. Why did Charles V fail to check the progress of Lutheranism in Germany?

Secondly, they may opt for 'To what extent' or 'How far' questions. In these one particular factor which prevented Charles from combating Lutheranism is identified, and you are asked to measure the importance of other factors against it. For example:

2. To what extent was it the German princes that prevented Charles V from suppressing Lutheranism in Germany?
3. How far was it Charles V's conflict with France that prevented him from dealing effectively with Protestantism in Germany?

Questions 1, 2 and 3 can be tackled in two ways – chronologically or thematically. If you follow a chronological approach it is essential that you do not just provide a simple narrative, but that you answer the question directly and analytically within your chronological framework (you will find some guidance on this on pages 81–2, which deals with essay-writing on the Habsburg–Valois rivalry). When you are dealing with the main chronological units of this topic (1519–21, 1521–41 and 1541–55) make sure that you consider the relative importance of different factors which you think help to explain Charles' failure to prevent the growth of Lutheranism, and base your conclusions on this.

'The Protestant Challenge' provides a good opportunity to escape from some of the restrictions of the chronological approach, and to adopt a more challenging analytical and thematic one. In answering questions on Charles' failure to suppress Lutheranism in Germany it is important that you start with a reliable list of all the major reasons for his failure, and that you can organise them into distinct themes. The following is a list of themes that might correspond with your paragraph headings:

a) Charles' personal failings as a ruler
b) The weakness of imperial authority
c) The political ambitions of the princes and the cities
d) Papal obstruction
e) Charles' other priorities and distractions
f) The popularity of Lutheranism in Germany

Question 1 could be answered in a series of 'because' paragraphs corresponding with these headings. Questions 2 and 3 require you, firstly, to assess how important the factor identified in the question is (the German princes or the conflict with France), and you should devote about a third of your essay to discussing it. Secondly, you must deal with other determinants and compare their importance with the factor identified in the question.

Finally, some questions on Charles V as Holy Roman Emperor focus on his political and constitutional disappointments, as well as his religious failures. For example:

4. How far was the ineffectiveness of Charles V in Germany due to the ambitions of the princes?

For this sort of question, follow the advice above, but make sure you deal adequately with political developments (covered in chapter 2).

2 The Muslim Challenge

As with your study of Charles' responses to the German Reformation, your understanding of the problems created for Charles by the Muslim challenge can be enhanced by wider reading on the nature of the challenge itself (see, for example, *The Ottoman Empire, 1450–1700* by Andrina Stiles, in this series). Questions that deal only with Charles and the Muslim challenge do appear in examinations, but they are not very common. Examiners, perhaps wrongly, do not usually accord as much importance to this area of Charles' activity as they do to some others. For this reason, the Muslim challenge is often combined with another aspect of Charles' reign. For example:

1. What problems did Charles V confront in Spain and the Mediterranean and how successful was he in overcoming them?
2. 'More than a match for the French, but impotent against Ottoman power.' To what extent is this a valid statement about the reign of Charles V?

Questions can extend beyond Charles' own reign. For example:

3. Assess the record of Charles V and his son, Philip II, in countering Ottoman power.

As you can see, a common focus of questions on 'The Muslim Challenge' is on the degree of success Charles experienced in this area. To answer such a question it is essential to have a good understanding of the nature of the problems Muslim powers posed to Charles and to Europe. This is discussed, in the context of the Mediterranean, on pages 99–101, and in the context of eastern Europe on page 107. Once you have clarified in your own mind what the scale of the problems were for Charles, you need to start collecting evidence which will demonstrate the extent to which he overcame them. It is best to organise your material in the same way as this section of the book, differentiating between the Mediterranean and the eastern European fronts. Then divide your evidence into two sections – successes and failures. This can be done with the help of a matrix. For example:

The Mediterranean		
date	*successes*	*failures*

Once you have organised your material in this way you should be in a good position to measure Charles' actions in meeting the Muslim challenge against the scale of the problems you identified above.

Source-based questions on 'Charles the Defender of the Faith'

1 Condemnations of heresy

Read the extract from Charles' statement to the Diet of Worms in 1521, on pages 86–7, and the extract from the Augsburg Recess in 1530, on page 89, and answer the following questions:

a) From the evidence of the extract on pages 86–7, why is Charles particularly concerned about the emergence of heresy in Germany? *(2 marks)*

b) In Charles' public statement on pages 86–7, what image is he trying to create of himself as Holy Roman Emperor? *(4 marks)*

c) From your own knowledge of Charles, why do you think he honoured his pledge of 'safe conduct' to Martin Luther (page 87)? (2 marks)

d) Describe the language and tone of the two extracts condemning Lutheranism? *(4 marks)*

e) What evidence do the two extracts provide of fears that religious heresy will be accompanied by social and political disruption? *(3 marks)*

2 Curbing the Emperor's crusading instincts

Read the extracts from the letters from Cardinal Tavera (page 102) and from Charles' sister Mary (page 104), and the extract from Charles' letter to his wife Isabella, and answer the following questions:

a) What arguments and techniques of persuasion are employed by Tavera and Mary to dissuade Charles from embarking on campaigns against his Muslim opponents? *(6 marks)*

b) What evidence is furnished in Charles' letter to Isabella of the difficulties of dissuading Charles from embarking on such ventures? *(4 marks)*

3 The Emperor Triumphant

Study the portrait of Charles on the cover, painted after the Battle of Mühlberg in 1547, and the painting on page 98 representing Charles' various triumphs. From your left to right are: the Sultan Suleiman the 'Magnificent', Pope Clement VII, Francis I and the three Protestant German princes, Duke William of Cleves, Duke Frederick of Saxony and Landgrave Philip of Hesse.

a) In what ways do the techniques employed by the two artists to portray a victorious Charles differ? Give reasons for your answer. *(6 marks)*

b) The two paintings can be described as Habsburg propaganda. What influence do you think they would have had at the time? *(4 marks)*

c) In what ways are the paintings useful to historians studying Charles V? *(5 marks)*

CHAPTER 5

Conclusion

1 Charles V and the Historians

Through the centuries there has been a large measure of scholarly agreement about the historical importance of Emperor Charles V. There are obvious reasons for this. In the first half of the sixteenth century he was the dominant prince of Christendom. He was very much 'centre-stage' in the great convulsions of the period – the Habsburg–Valois wars and the German Reformation. His empire was so extensive that there were few areas of Christendom where his influence was not felt, and the legacy of his reign helped to shape the history of Europe for generations. Thus the biographer Royall Tyler concluded, with some justification, that 'For a thousand years, from Charlemagne to Napoleon, no other ruler mattered so much to Christendom.' However, it would be very difficult to sustain the argument that Charles established his historical importance by the exertion of his individual will on political affairs, as might be said of a Napoleon or a Hitler. Rather, his importance lies in the unparalleled power and responsibility he inherited through birth. Furthermore, historians nowadays tend to reject the 'great man' school of history, which too readily ascribes historical change to the decisions and actions of individual rulers. They insist that the actions of major historical personalities must be weighed in importance against wider and longer-term social, economic and political factors. We have seen a good example of this in debates about the origins of the *Communeros* Revolt in Spain; was it triggered by the arrival of a distrusted foreign monarch, as some more traditional histories maintain, or do its origins lie in longer-term and more impersonal factors (see pages 25–6). In the historical literature on Charles V it is usually biographies that are most prone to present an exaggerated picture of the emperor's historical impact. Naturally, they focus on Charles' personal role, since this is their subject, at the expense of wider historical processes. Indeed, although this book is not a conventional biography of Charles, it is likely to have the kind of 'structural bias' as other biographies. Readers should try to assess critically how decisive an impact the emperor had on the events in which he was caught up.

Charles exhibited many qualities as a ruler and statesman which have been admired by generations of historians. His openness to criticism has commonly been noted. In Spain, the Netherlands and Germany he tolerated frequent and untramelled criticism of his policies from his advisers and leading subjects. He has also been commended by some historians for his sense of justice and sense of proportion in punishing disloyalty.⌉'Bloodthirstiness', according to Edward Armstrong, 'was unknown to Charles'. He was genuinely saddened when French provocation forced him to visit war upon Christendom, and in his punishment of the Ghent and *Communeros* rebellions, it has been contended, he was more anxious to deter future revolt than to exact vengeance on the rebels. He has also received the approbation of some commentators for displaying considerable skills of improvisation and flexibility in political affairs. For example, despite his deep-seated hostility to Lutheranism, he was prepared to make concessions to the Protestants in order to win them back to a reformed Catholicism, or simply to obtain German aid against the Ottoman threat. When his dynastic scheme to ensure Philip's succession as Holy Roman Emperor broke down in the 1550s, he quickly attempted to snatch victory from the jaws of defeat by arranging Philip's marriage to Mary Tudor. Underlying this capacity to adapt to changing circumstances some historians have identified an essential pragmatism and realism in the Emperor's political outlook. Politics was the art of the possible. As a ruler he chose to govern his dominions in conformity with their existing laws and customs, as to attempt to do otherwise would only antagonise vested political interests. As a dynast he curtailed his family ambitions in England and the northern kingdoms in order to safeguard Habsburg trading interests. In the words of the biographer Fernandez Alvarez he 'cut his suit according to his cloth'. Paradoxically, perhaps, another virtue that is commonly recognised in Charles as a ruler was his fixity of purpose and the constancy of his aims. To argue that he was also flexible and pragmatic might appear to contradict this. However, the two qualities can be reconciled if it is accepted that Charles was adaptable in the tactics he employed in the pursuit of his long-term and unalterable aims. It should be clear from this book that it is quite possible to argue that Charles' longer-term aims did remain notably resolute. Despite all the difficulties he faced, he sought to preserve his inheritance, to safeguard Catholicism and to challenge the forces of Islam. If such a portrayal of the Emperor is accepted, then his conciliatory policy towards Lutheranism in Germany does not, in the last analysis, denote any sacrifice of principle. Rather it shows a willingness to try every possible expedient to achieve his goal of reunifying Christendom. Historians have not only been impressed by the steadfastness of Charles' aims, but many have taken note of the earnest sense of duty and responsibility with which he pursued them. Despite the formidable odds he faced, and despite the limitations of his intellect and ability perceived by numerous writers, he persevered and struggled dutifully to fulfil his obligations as he saw them. As one of his biographers concludes, he 'did his duty according to his lights, worked doggedly and was harder on himself than on others'.

Such, then, were the Emperor's strengths as a ruler. But how do historians assess his actual achievements? It is only to be expected that most historians view the past from the perspective of the present, and that historical judgements are rooted in the climate of the times in which they are made. Thus recent historians have tended to view the reign of Charles V from the point of view of the modern nation-state which has been in the ascendant from the nineteenth century onwards. Hence evaluations of his reign often focus upon the impact he had on his individual dominions and how this affected their development into the unified nations of modern times. However, it should, of course, be borne in mind that Charles himself had no conception of his dominions as embryonic nation-states. As Fernandez Alvarez emphasises, 'Charles was a continental, rather than a national figure. He belonged to none of his dominions'. Nevertheless, his role in the evolution of modern state structures was historically important. Thus historians of the Netherlands have generally been generous to Charles V, stressing his contribution to the development of its administration and, in particular, to its independence from the Holy Roman Empire. Similarly, he has been highly esteemed in Spanish historiography. Historians have given their approval to his continuation of the bureaucratic, or 'conciliar', reforms initiated by Ferdinand and Isabella before him. They have also noted with some satisfaction the extent to which Spain increasingly formed the centre of gravity in Charles' empire and, more specifically, how he achieved Spanish hegemony in Italy.

Of course, the Emperor's responsibilities extended beyond those of a territorial ruler. Despite varying degrees of national bias, historians have identified significant areas of success in his more supranational role as a dynast and a 'Defender of the Faith'. As a dynast, it has been argued that Charles came away with the richest prizes in the Habsburg–Valois wars and that he paved the way for a more peaceful coexistence with France after his death. It has also been contended that he achieved notable successes in his family ambitions. For Karl Brandi, for example, ensuring the future greatness of the House of Habsburg was his crowning achievement. H. G. Koenigsberger sums up his dynastic success: 'He had successfully defended all he had been granted and often he had extended it'. As a 'Defender of the Faith' he has been given credit for fortifying Catholicism in Christendom during a period of great vulnerability and crisis. The Netherlands were protected from heresy, at least during Charles' reign. And of the Spanish empire, an American historian has commented: 'At the time of his abdication, no other country of Western Europe, save Portugal, was so free from the taint of heresy as were the different scattered territories that comprised the Spanish Empire'. Even in Germany he laboured to defend Catholicism, and he has been associated with the survival of Catholicism in significant parts of the Empire. Finally, he consistently put pressure on the papacy to reform abuses within the Church through the convocation of a General Council. Substantial reform only came after his death. However, some historians attribute some of the achievements of the

Tapestry depicting Charles in retirement at Yuste

Church in the second half of the sixteenth century to the earlier promptings of Emperor Charles. It has also been claimed that Charles made an important contribution to protecting Christendom from the forces of Islam. None would claim that he defeated this foe, but some assert that he at least contained the threat. As G. R. Elton points out: 'Of all the many politicians who talked about the Turkish danger and vaguely appealed to Christendom to unite against it, he was the only one willing to translate words into action'.

The historical writing on Charles V does, however, contain criticisms of his qualities as a political leader. Some maintain that the Emperor was often over-dependent on advisers and members of his family. According to this analysis, he lacked the skills and strength of character to provide unified leadership for his empire. In the 1520s there is evidence that he was somewhat in thrall to Mercurino Gattinara. For long periods the internal affairs of Spain, the Netherlands and Germany appear to have been guided not by the Emperor, but by his appointed deputies and advisers. In the 1550s there is little doubt that he became worn-out by his political responsibilities and difficulties. This led him to give up Germany as a lost cause and to hand it over completely to Ferdinand. Historians have also interpreted his career as betraying a debilitating irresolution and indecisiveness. From this perspective, he often seems to have clutched at any excuse to avoid decisions. Hence he was frequently thrown off his chosen course by the tide of events. His delays in the 1540s and 1550s in sorting out how his empire was to be divided between Philip and Ferdinand served only to intensify his dynastic difficulties. Above all, in Germany his responses to Lutheranism can be construed as weak and vacillating, as he alternated between a policy of appeasement towards Lutheranism and a desire to compel obedience to Catholicism.

A further criticism that is sometimes levelled against Charles is that once he had made up his mind about something he could be stubborn and unwilling to yield to good advice. Some of his crusading ventures against Muslim forces in the Mediterranean were carried out against the insistent advice of his closest advisers. His obstinacy resulted in the disastrous campaign against Algiers in 1541. Charles' campaigns against his Muslim rivals also cast the gravest doubt on the assertions of some historians that he was forgiving and peace-loving by nature. His brutality against the 'Infidel' is evident in his treatment of the inhabitants of Tunis in 1535 (see page 102). However, even with his own Christian subjects he found it difficult to forgive disloyalty, and a strong element of vindictiveness has been detected in his punishment of the rebellious town of Ghent in 1540. Karl Brandi, among others, has noted that his sense of anger and bitterness at what he perceived to be any betrayal grew more violent and deep-seated as he grew older. A more fundamental allegation against Charles as a ruler is that he was lacking in vision and imagination. He was conservative by instinct and showed little aptitude for innovation and reform, as his reliance on time-worn methods of governing Germany seems to prove. Similarly, he has been criticised for failing to develop any centralised mechanisms for administering his empire as a whole. In addition, H. G. Koenigsberger points out that he failed to elaborate any coherent imperial economic policy, or even to conceive of the need for one. From this point of view, he failed to display initiative in dealing with the problems he faced. He was, therefore, forced to react to events, rather than control them. 'From first to last,' Edward Armstrong argues, 'his action was defensive, forced upon him by the movements of his enemies.'

There has always been an acknowledgement that Charles V's reign contained important disappointments. The Emperor himself helped to generate such an image of failure by declaring publicly that he retired from office conscious of his own deficiencies and saddened by the frustration of his hopes (see page 1). Certainly, when historians have measured his actions against his own aims and ambitions his failures have appeared particularly evident. He wished to recreate the Christian triumphs of the Crusades against Islam, but signally failed to do so. He wanted to unite Christendom under the Pope's, and his own, leadership. Instead, his relations with the papacy were invariably strained, whilst he was intermittently at war with the Catholic monarchs of France. In Germany, the Emperor wished to re-establish unitary political leadership, or so he said at the Diet of Worms in 1521 (see page 37), but, in the face of the political ambitions of the German princes, he failed miserably. Moreover, his commitment to Catholic universalism was disappointed most of all in Germany, where a permanent schism and a dangerous source of heresy emerged. Finally, as a proud dynast his inability to pass on his empire undivided to his son was a severe disappointment to his family ambitions. Perhaps, as G. R. Elton among others has observed, his ambitions were 'extravagant'.

Other historiographical criticisms levelled against Charles focus upon the long-term consequences of his policies. Spain may have been successfully protected from Protestantism, but from the time of Charles the country became dangerously insulated from European thought and learning. Some argue that his suppression of Protestantism in the Netherlands brought about a backlash of extreme Protestantism in the reign of Philip II. It can also be maintained that in dynastic politics the House of Habsburg was significantly weakened when Charles' empire was divided, as subsequent Habsburg Emperors in Germany were deprived of aid and support from Spain and the Netherlands. In addition, Charles' own imperial reign confirmed the tendencies of the Empire towards disintegration, and doomed it to a future of internal conflict and international impotence. However, it is the economic legacy that Charles bequeathed to his successors that has been most commonly criticised by historians. H. G. Koenigsberger, for example, for example, refers to 'horrendous bills', and M. L. Salgado expands this point with particular vigour – 'The extent to which Charles had mortgaged or sold his patrimony was spectacular, and was generally considered unprecedented.' She further argues that such financial irresponsibility bred mounting resentment against Habsburg rule and damaged the future stability of his dominions. In the Netherlands, in particular, there was a widespread feeling that their assets had been stripped to serve Spanish interests. Anti-Spanish feelings came to the surface violently in the reign of Philip II.

There are some historians who readily acknowledge the failures of Charles' reign but are reluctant to attach too much of the blame to the emperor himself. They contend that Charles inherited so many responsibilities as a ruler and a statesman that they were impossible for one man to discharge effectively. His obligations as a territorial ruler were awesome in themselves, even without the wider duties he incurred as head of the Habsburg dynasty and Holy Roman Emperor. It is certainly impossible to observe any of his actions without being struck by the immense difficulty he had in concentrating on a single issue without being distracted by other pressing problems. Hence, even his moments of triumph, like that in 1526 against the French and that in 1547 against the German Protestants, were invariably short-lived. Royall Tyler comments: 'The means at his disposal to face the demands upon him always fell short of what he needed to exploit a victory or a diplomatic triumph.'

An interesting explanation for the sense of failure which so often surrounds Charles is the 'Charles as anachronism' approach. Numerous historians have been struck by the fact that Charles appears very much a medieval figure in an increasingly modern world. As such, it is argued, he was destined to failure as his actions were out of tune with the realities of his day. There is significant evidence that 'He belonged essentially to an age now dead' (Karl Brandi). He took little interest in the classical revivalism and the 'New Learning' of the European Renaissance of his time. His values were rooted in the teachings of the medieval Church and in the chivalric romances of the middle ages. He clung to the medieval ideal of Catholic universalism at the very time when the authority of the Church was rejected by the Protestant movement. As a fervent opponent of Protestantism, he has been portrayed, particularly by Protestant historians, as opposing religious ideas better suited to the modern age. His dream of military triumph over the forces of Islam has been interpreted as a throw-back to the medieval concept of the 'Crusade'. Very few other princes of Christendom paid anything more than lip-service to the spirit of the Crusades. Lastly, some historians maintain that in politics Charles was out of tune with the modern ideology of the nation-state and nationhood which was emerging in Europe during this period. Instead, he idealised the out-dated supranational authorities of medieval Christendom – the Pope and the Holy Roman Emperor.

The 'Charles as anachronism' perspective is attractive as it appears to provide an explanation as to why the Emperor's career is so often associated with failure. However, important qualifications to this thesis have been advanced. Firstly, it has been proposed that it exaggerates the processes of change and 'modernity' in Charles' time, and, that it under-estimates the important continuities his age shared with the middle ages. For example, most historians nowadays would be very cautious about locating the emergence of the modern nation state in Charles' time when medieval notions of dynastic sovereignty were just as potent. Secondly, it can be contended that Charles did, in significant respects, adapt his outlook to the changes of his day. In Spain and the Netherlands, for example, he took administrative reform in the direction of bureaucratic modernisation. To this extent, then, he assumed 'both an archaic and a modern air' (Fernandez Alvarez) and, in this he was surely representative of his age.

Making notes on 'Conclusion'

This chapter summarises the varying views of historians about Emperor Charles and outlines a range of interpretations, some of which contradict each other. You will no doubt agree with some of the judgements and disagree with others. The most important thing is for you to make up your own mind about Charles' record. So, in taking notes on this chapter, try to include your own ideas and illustrations as well as those of historians. The following questions should assist you:

1. Was Charles as important as Armstrong asserts?
2. What were Charles' positive personal qualities?
3. What were Charles' achievements?
4. What were Charles' negative personal qualities?
5. What were Charles' disappointments and failures?
6. How convincing are the following explanations for Charles' failures:
   a) the nature of his inheritance and responsibilities
   b) having over-ambitious aims
   c) 'Charles as anachronism'?

Answering general essay questions on Charles V

General questions covering the overall role and responsibilities of Charles V are not uncommon. Such questions present particular challenges. Consult page 46 for advice on planning general questions on Charles as a territorial ruler. However some questions go further than this and allow you to deal with his other responsibilities as a dynast and as a 'Defender of the Faith'. For example:

1. To what extent did Charles V fulfil his most important aims?

General questions on Charles V should encourage you to reflect upon the Emperor's life and career as a whole and to come to thoughtful historical judgements about his overall significance and achievements. It is difficult to anticipate the particular 'slant' of such questions, but it is vital to think carefully about the precise wording of this sort of question and to relate your answer very closely to it. You must avoid the temptation to 'regurgitate' a rehearsed survey of Charles' career regardless of the question.

General questions often invite you to consider a statement or a judgement about Charles' record. These can be in the form of a challenging statement. For example:

2. 'Successful everywhere except in Germany.' Discuss this view of Charles V.

Remember that you do not have to agree with any assertion or quotation provided by the examiners; you may disagree in part or entirely, although it is possible that you may be in complete agreement.

It is not feasible to provide examples of every possible type of overview question on Charles. However, it is realistic to illustrate some of the more common approaches. Firstly, examiners sometimes focus on the problems and difficulties which Charles faced. For example:

3. Which of Charles V's responsibilities caused him the most difficulties?

A variation on this theme requires you to assess the extent to which Charles' difficulties were inescapable or were the result of his own actions. For example:

4. To what extent were Charles V's problems of his own making?

Secondly, questions sometimes focus on Charles' aims and objectives. See question 1 and for example:

5. With what justification can it be argued that Charles V's aims were over-ambitious?

Thirdly, you might well be invited to assess Charles' successes and failures. This could involve measuring his success against his own aims and objectives. For example, again see question 1. In some ways this question is quite straightforward as you are provided with a yardstick (his most important aims) against which to measure his success. However, some questions are less specific about the criteria you should use to evaluate success and failure. For example:

6. To what extent was Charles V only successful as King of Spain?

In such a question you should think about Charles' successes and failures, firstly in the context of his aims and objectives. You must avoid anachronistic historical judgements, where Charles' record is assessed by criteria which are not appropriate to the time in which he lived. For example, he can hardly be blamed for failing to transform his inheritance into nation-states as the idea of the nation-state did not really exist in his day (see page 126). However, do remember that historians have the benefit of hindsight, and that you can legitimately judge Charles' career in the light of the long-term consequences of his actions. For example, in assessing Charles' financial policies in Spain and the Netherlands you should consider his financial legacies in both countries (see pages 33–4 and page 20).

Finally, some questions require you to evaluate Charles' personal qualities as a political leader and as an international statesman. For example:

7. How far do you think Charles V was a man of moderate and limited talents?

The examples given above are arranged so as to differentiate between main types of overview questions on Charles V. However, in practice different approaches can be combined in the same question. For example:

8. What were Charles V's greatest failures and to what extent were they due to his own limitations?

Try to compose some other questions which combine several approaches to overview questions.

Further Reading

There is something of a shortage of worthwhile and readily accessible books on Charles V. The best is:

Martyn Rady, *The Emperor Charles V* (Longman, 1988)

It is short, easily obtained and contains many telling insights. However it is weighted towards Charles' role in Germany and suffers from too chronological an approach. The same author has written a brief and interesting article comparing Charles' reign with his brother Ferdinand's:

Martyn Rady, 'The Emperors Charles V and Ferdinand I', *History Sixth*, 9 (March 1991)

If at all possible consult:

H. G. Koenigsberger, 'The Empire of Charles V in Europe', *The New Cambridge Modern History*, vol ii 2nd edition (CUP, 1990)

(This article is little changed from that in the first edition which might be more readily available in libraries.) This is an excellent article by a leading historian. The same author has published a concise and easily digested survey of Charles' reign:

H. G. Koenigsberger, 'The Emperor Charles V', *History Sixth*, 4 (May 1989)

If you have time to read a full biography, the least arduous and most up-to-date is:

M. Fernandez Alvarez, *Charles V: Elected Emperor and Hereditary Ruler* (Thames and Hudson, 1975)

It provides good material on both Charles' personal and public lives, although it does have a clear Spanish 'slant'.

British historians have written some highly-acclaimed histories of early modern Spain. The following are best on Charles as King of Spain, but also provide useful material on Charles' wider responsibilities:

J. H. Elliot, *Imperial Spain, 1469–1716* (Edward Arnold, 1963)
Henry Kamen, *Spain, 1469–1716: A Society of Conflict* (Longman, 1983)
A. W. Lovett, *Early Habsburg Spain, 1517–1598* (OUP, 1986)
John Lynch, *Spain under the Habsburgs*, vol i: *Empire and Absolutism, 1516–1598* (Blackwell, 1964)

The older (and longer) biographies of Charles V do not really merit close reading unless you are engaged in an in-depth study. However, they may be worth dipping into:

Edward Armstrong, *The Emperor Charles V*, 2 vols (MacMillan, 1901)
Karl Brandi, *The Emperor Charles V* (Jonathan Cape, 1939)
Royall Tyler, *The Emperor Charles V* (Allen and Unwin, 1956)

A specialist work which only deals with a short period of Charles' reign is worth consulting briefly for its robust criticism of the Emperor:

M. J. Salgado, *The Changing Face of Empire: Charles V, Philip II and Habsburg Authority, 1551–1559* (CUP, 1988)

Salgado has also written a detailed and valuable essay on the Habsburg–Valois rivalry in the second edition of *The New Cambridge Modern History* referred to above.

Finally, two rather different general surveys of sixteenth-century European history are particularly good on Charles V:

G. R. Elton, *Reformation Europe, 1517–1559* (Fontana, 1963)

Now something of a 'classic', it is full of shrewd judgements. Use the index if you do not have time for a leisurely read.

Katherine Brice has written a concise, well-organised and reliable chapter in:

John Lotherington (ed), *Years of Renewal: European History, 1470–1600* (Hodder & Stoughton, 1988)

Sources on Charles V

There are no easily obtainable collections of sources in English except:

Martyn Rady, *The Emperor Charles V* (Longman, 1988)

There are nineteen documents at the end of this book.

A wide variety of visual sources is included in:

M. Fernandez Alvarez, *Charles V: Elected Emperor and Hereditary Ruler* (Thames and Hudson, 1975)

Acknowledgements

The Publishers would like to thank the following for permission to reproduce material in this volume:

Allen & Unwin (now Unwin Hyman of HarperCollins Publishers Limited) for the extract from Royall Tyler *The Emperor Charles Fifth* (Allen and Unwin, 1956); Basil Blackwell for the extracts from John Lynch *Spain under the Habsburgs* (Blackwell, 1986) and C. R. N. Routh *They saw it happen in Europe* (Blackwell, 1965); Edward Arnold (Publishers) Limited for the extract from J. H. Elliot, *Imperial Spain* (Penguin, 1983); Thames & Hudson Ltd for the extract from M. Fernandez Alverez *Charles V* (Thames & Hudson, 1975).

Every effort has been made to trace and acknowledge ownership of copyright. The publishers will be glad to make suitable arrangements with any copyright holders whom it has not been possible to contact.

The Publishers would also like to thank the following for permission to reproduce copyright illustrations in this volume:

Museo del Prado, Madrid/Ampliaciones y Reproducciones "MAS" cover; Kunsthistorisches Museum, Vienna page 5; Rijksmuseum-Stichting, Amsterdam page 18, page 60; The British Library page 98; Collection Musée du Temps, Palais Granvelle, Besançon/Photo Studio Granvelle, Besançon page 122.

Index

Readers seeking a specific piece of information might find it helpful to consult the table of *Contents* as well as this brief *Index*.